BUSKER

THE LIFE AND TIMES OF
A MODERN TIRE TRAMP

D.B. ROUSE

dbrouse.com, pintorouse@gmail.com

Second Edition

Editor: Brendan Shea, brendansheamusic.com
Cover and Book Layout: Austin Meyers, ak5a.com

A big thanks to Brendan Shea for whose input and having taken on the role of my editor made this possible. See his words and hear his music at: brendansheamusic.com

I'd like to thank Austin L. Meyers (AK5A) whose technological know-how and graphic intuition brought this project to the next level. See his multimedia arts at: ak5a.com

And a big thanks to Rod Kouba and Blake Langlinais for participating in this madness and giving me permission to publish their words in the epilogue.

Printed in the USA

ISBN-13: 978-1481199834
ISBN-10: 1481199838

To my parents, who never disowned me.

Busk, *verb*

The action of playing a musical instrument, usually on street corners, in a possible exchange for tips, services, or goods; friendships often result.

Ex.:

1.   I went downtown to busk because if I don't make any money, my girlfriend will leave me and I will die of starvation.

2.   I will busk the shit out of this place.

Other than being Elvis Presley, all I ever wanted to do was play music and travel. So the question was, how does one travel around making music and still manage to survive and support oneself without any music business connections, or really any business sense whatsoever? I couldn't think of an answer, so I decided to just go out and do it, hopefully figuring things out as I went along.

I also had a notion that there would be cities somewhere that I could turn into base camps and call home. I burned through thousands of gallons of gas, trying to find these cities and make their downtowns my playgrounds.

The following is based on true events that occurred between 2007 and 2012. At times, for the sake of the text, I combined a few people or locations into one person or place. At times, I've told my imagination where to begin then allowed it to run wild. Librarians should file this work under partial-fiction. The names of certain people, places, and companies have been changed to protect the innocent and the guilty. Except my name; that one stayed the same, and you can be the judge of my innocence.

- D.B. Rouse

ROAD SONG

I was dreaming I was on a boat - a boat on the salty luke-warm stew of the Atlantic - busily doing absolutely nothing. I could hear the waves gently pounding the side of the boat. It was as though I had stuck my head inside a seashell and fell asleep. The ocean slowly rocked me awake, and I found I was not in a boat, but actually stretched out awkwardly across the front seats of my minivan.

For the last couple days I had been sleeping there, at a rest stop forty miles west of Nashville. The sun was just starting to rise over the hood of the van. Oddly enough, I could still hear ocean waves gently swishing against the vehicle. As my vision came into focus, I saw that it wasn't ocean waves at all. It was in fact a raggedy homeless man wiping down my windshield. I scowled at him, and shook my head 'No. No business here, buddy.'

He moved on to the next parked vehicle. Maybe he was hard up for money to put toward his first drink of the day; maybe he just liked watching people sleep. Either way, I passed out again. I needed rest. Besides, I had a boat I wanted to get back to.

I had gotten into Nashville a few days earlier. I was thinking about moving there eventually but wanted to get to know the place before I made any plans. All I was certain of at that point was that I was very uncertain about Nashville. I wandered around downtown aimlessly for several days. I took in the lights, the crowds, the vibe. I meandered through ancient libraries and played open mics.

Nashville was a lot like how I pictured L.A., except that instead of everyone in town being an aspiring or burnt out actor, people here were all burnt out or aspiring musicians, like me. For instance, I traded CDs with the security guard at the bank.

After another day and another round of open mics among musicians who were trying to be pop star stereotypes, I gave up the ghost and decided that my heart wasn't in Nashville. That I should try to peddle my talents, or delusions of talent, elsewhere. But my feet were dragging. I had really been hoping this would be the place for me, that I would feel at home here, that I would be discovered overnight without putting any effort into it and start a rigorous national tour schedule. Honestly, I still hope for overnight success, even if that night is actually thirty or forty years of hard work.

So my big clumsy feet were dragging and would not let me leave town. Instead, they brought me downtown to Broadway, where I opened my guitar case and started to busk for bread.

I started at 10 AM that day. Almost immediately I became something of a tourist attraction. Maybe my look had a bit to do with it. This was my first music-hobo trip and I had weird hygiene rules. I thought I would somehow be more marketable as a street musician if I was clean-shaven, had short hair, and wore a dress jacket and a nice shirt. I looked like an illegitimate son of Hank Williams.

People would crowd around me while I was playing and get their pictures taken. I couldn't help laughing as I pictured myself in all these strangers' pictures, projected life-size up on a wall of some family's Nashville slideshow.

"This one was taken on Broadway downtown. In Nashville, the natives play music on the street corners!" the narrator would say, while audience members were falling asleep or plotting an exit.

It really did wonders for my ego, like I was on my way to

becoming a star or something. They'd drop a dollar into my guitar case and then inevitably ask me a question that would shatter the illusion.

"Where's the Country Music Hall of Fame from here?"

"I don't know. I just got into town a few days ago."

"Oh. Where are you from?"

"Wisconsin," I'd reply, and they would all walk away, probably feeling they had been conned out of a dollar and a photo by a fast-talking Yankee.

A little girl of about three or four walked by, stopped, and listened to me in an entranced state for two entire songs. Her parents cooed and took photos the whole time. By the end of the second song I had attracted a full mob of grandmothers, like they had all formed a gang and started roaming the streets in search of babies and soft food. After I had lost the little girl's attention and she went off with her family, the whole cheek-pinching bunch pinched their purses and tipped me, generously. I put serious thought into running after that little girl, giving her a cut of the money, and setting up a deal with her in which she would stop by every few hours and listen to a couple songs. Maybe I could make it in this town yet.

Shortly after that, a Willie Nelson look-a-like walked by. He led a different walking tour past every hour or so. He would stop the tours right next to me as I played and tell people, "Here in Nashville there is an old tradition of musicians busking on Broadway. Oftentimes they play here for sixteen hours a day, as it is their only source of income." He then led the tourists past single file; some of his clients even tipped.

Financially speaking, Willie's look-a-like had me pegged. Busking had become my sole income source. I had quit my job, my life, and taken to the road to make music: a romantic-sounding suicide and rebirth. It would become a lot less romantic and wonderfully, terribly real before too long. But it sure didn't feel real here. That's because Nashville isn't a town, it's an amusement park. On that day I was just an old-fashioned carnie, juggling reality and illusion for tourists who preferred the illusion.

There was a twenty-something hobo type who passed my corner sidewalk stage every once in a while. He was a larger fellow, with a long dreadlock mullet and a giant rucksack on his back. He had slightly sunken, lively eyes framed by a stubbly face and short bangs. Every time he passed he would stop and sing along to whatever I was playing.

He was passing me for the fifth time at about 2 PM that day. I had just finished a song and was thinking about calling it quits when he asked, "You want a beer?"

Hell yes I did. "Hell yes," I said.

"Cool. I'll go grab some and come back in a few."

Off he went. I continued busking, figuring he'd be back shortly. After a parched hour, he made it back and said, "I got kicked out of Coyote's, but I got two twenty-four-ounce cans of Ice House from the store next to them."

I paused. Were we going to drink these in public, right there on Broadway? And who was this guy anyway? Why should I even trust him?

Because he had beer, that's why. He raised the bag with the beverages up and said, "We should drink these over in the park at the end of the street."

"Okay," I replied.

"My name is John the Firetruck," he said as I put my guitar away.

"Nice to meet you Mr. Firetruck. I'm D.B. Rouse."

We set off walking toward the park wedged between the end of Broadway and the Cumberland River. "How long you been here, D.B.?" he drawled.

"About a week. You?"

"Well I got here yesterday morning. I was trying to get to Alabama. Turns out the train I hopped was going here instead."

We were weaving in and out of tourist traps. Get your "old-timey" photo taken. Get your Nashville shot glass, thimble, or spoon. Have a caricature of yourself drawn. Ahead of us I saw a bald man sitting on the sidewalk with a live monkey on his shoulder. For a little cash, you could get your picture taken with it. Nothing says Nashville like this man's monkey.

When John saw the Monkey Man he turned to me, dreadlocked mullet swinging in the wind, and said excitedly, "You gotta meet this guy. He is so cool."

When we got close to the Monkey Man he jumped to his feet, pointed at John, and screamed, "The cops!"

John and I stopped in our tracks. The monkey darted behind his owner's giant, bald head in search of cover.

"The cops are looking for you, you son of a bitch!" the Monkey Man continued yelling at John. He was beginning to draw in tourists. "I don't know what you were on last night, but people had to hold me back. I was going to strangle you. You don't go around saying shit like that here - not in Nashville."

John the Firetruck calmly walked over to him, looked him square in the eyes and said, "Judge not, and you will not be judged. Condemn not, and you will not be condemned. Forgive and you will be forgiven. Luke six, thirty-seven."

Then John walked on past him, and I quickly followed. The Monkey Man's eyes burned a hole in John's dreadlocks, and the confused tourists scattered.

"I see you've gotten to know the locals," I said to him after walking in silence for a while.

"Yeah." He looked into space thoughtfully. "I don't remember what he's talking about. I woke up under a bridge at three o'clock this morning, stone-cold sober."

We ducked behind a wall in the park and cracked open our beer. About forty yards to the left of us, the shadiest, most desperate and lowdown-looking group of street people I had ever seen milled about in a circle. They were skinny as rails and caked in grime. Their eyes were sunken and had dark circles around them, like they were looking out of a cave. Their clothing was in tatters and gave them the general appearance of medieval peasants with the Black Plague.

"Steer clear of them," John said nodding in their direction. "They drink Listerine. I tried it with them once, but never again. I'm a bit of a drunk, but give strong drink to him who is perishing, and wine to those who are bitter of heart. Let him drink and forget his poverty. Proverbs thirty-one, six."

I got the feeling that he used some of these Bible passages a lot. I also had the feeling that he was just making things up and attributing them to the Bible.

"John!" a gruff voice shouted from down a ways. I turned and saw two more hobos sitting against the wall. They seemed closer to the John variety than the Listerine-drinking kind. The fellow yelling at John had about half of a skinny joint in his hand and was waving us over with it. We got up, toting guitar and beer, walked around some tourists, and followed the pungent smell to its source.

"Hey John, how are you?" said the older hobo, passing him the joint.

"Better now," John replied.

The two hobos looked up at me, sizing me and my suit up.

"Hi. I'm D.B. I just hit the road the other day, and I've decided to be a hobo," I explained.

The older one, who looked a lot like a philosophy professor I had in a past life, chuckled and said to himself, "A self-made hobo..."

The younger one, who seemed about John's age, said, "Well, hi D.B. I'm Dan. You know where I can find some crack?"

"No. I uhh... just got here a few days ago."

He grinned an unshaven grin at me. "So you want to be a hobo? What train did you come into town on?"

"Actually, I drove here. I have a van."

"Then you're not a hobo at all," Dan said. "You're what they call a tire tramp. Mind if I pluck your guitar?"

I popped open my guitar case and pulled out my Taylor. "Now Dan," I said, still holding the guitar, "this guitar is my one and only. I've named her Meal-ticket..."

"I get it, I get it. I'll be gentle with her," Dan said and grabbed Meal-ticket out of my hands.

We all sat around listening as he busted out a handful of hard-drinking, curse-filled, drugged-out Hank III songs.

The Professor turned to me. "So you've decided to be a

hobo? I don't know anyone who would choose to live like this."

I thought about this for a moment. "Well it seems like a kind of simple and carefree way to go about life," I said, with Woody Guthrie and Jack Kerouac ideals rattling around loosely in my head.

"Kid," Professor started, with Dan singing a song about crack in the background. "I'm fifty-seven years old. Most days I'm lucky to get a good meal if I ain't sifting through garbage. I once had a great job, a wife, and a family. I see them everywhere I go. I'm from Nevada, see," he took an expired Nevada license out of his pocket. "And I'm actually slowly making my way back there. I woke up one morning in Reno, deathly hungover, penniless after a night of gambling. My life's savings, my family's well-being thrown away like so much Monopoly money in the wind. I couldn't go back to my family. I couldn't face them like that. So here I am, four years later."

Dan had stopped playing and he handed Meal-ticket back to me. He scratched the side of his head vigorously, raising a small cloud of dust. "Is anyone else here literally itching for crack?" he asked.

I strummed my guitar gently as John offered Dan a cigarette. He offered me and the Professor one as well, but I passed.

"I'm trying to kick the habit too," John said, lighting one. "I'm just waiting on that ten-day sentence so I can come out clean."

The Professor lit his cigarette and asked, "Mind if I play a few songs on your Meal-ticket there?"

"Sure," I said and handed it to him.

The Professor played 'Stairway' and 'Turn the Page' before handing me back my guitar.

"I'm sorry I bled all over your guitar, man," he said. His strumming thumb had ripped open at some point. His splattered blood was drying on Meal-ticket as I put it away.

John crushed his empty beer can. "I think we need more beer," he said.

"Should we vote to see who makes the next beer run?" Dan

asked, looking directly at me.

"No. I'll take care of this round," the Professor said.

I split when the Professor did, us going opposite ways. I found my van and drove forty miles west to my parking spot at the rest stop. It's the space right in front of the "No Overnight Parking" sign.

I woke up from a bad dream that I immediately forgot. That morning brought no strange visitors to clean my windshield. Through the smudges and dead bugs on the glass, I could see an overcast summer day beginning.

I drove back into Nashville and busked at my corner. Things were slow. People passed by quickly. I barely had any money in my case when he came along.

I could smell him before I saw him. He smelled like Everclear and moonshine stills exploding in the Tennessee hills. He was a grizzled old man wearing a cowboy hat and leather vest, and he was stumbling towards me.

I remember thinking to myself 'This guy seems awfully drunk for 11 AM. Maybe I should play him a drinking song.'

I was about to play 'Tear in my Beer' when he stopped two feet in front of me and asked, "Are you an angel, son?"

"Excuse me?"

He took a step forward, bloodshot eyes burning into mine. "You look like an angel, son. Are you an angel?"

"No. No, no," I said, shaking my head and taking a step back. "I'm real and alive. I'm also a black belt in Karate," I lied.

He took another step closer. "It's just... I heard you singing. And then I saw you, and you gotta be an angel."

I tried to take another step back, but was blocked by a building. "Nope. You are mistaken." I was looking for an escape route. I knew I could dash either left or right, but the guitar would be an issue, and I'd have to leave the case.

'Wait - there is nothing to worry about here,' I rationalized to myself. 'It's downtown Nashville, bustling with people in broad daylight. He's not going to try to pull anything. Stay calm.'

He took another big step toward me, our faces almost touching. "You must be an angel," he insisted. His moon-shine-soaked words brushed the skin of my cheek. I could see every horrible syllable before it came out of his scattered yellow teeth.

'Shit,' I thought. 'So this is how it ends.' He was going to pull a knife and make an angel out of me yet.

He continued, "See, I had a son 'bout your age, 'bout your height. Had your eyes and big nose too."

"Well I'm not him. I'm D.B. Rouse, from Wisconsin."

"My son," he went on without blinking, "just died in Iraq."

"I'm terribly sorry to hear that, sir," I said.

He stuck his hand out to shake mine. He had a grip like a vise.

"My son played music too. Now you play."

I broke into a shaky version of 'On the Road Again' as the old man took a welcome step back. He started hitting his leg in time, and then pulled a harmonica out of his vest. We weren't in the same key but he kept squealing away on it, stopping every so often to mutter something about angels.

After I finished that song, he snatched my guitar pick from my hand and tossed it into the street. Then he pulled out a thin wallet, found something in it and pressed it into my palm.

"There. That's better," he said.

I looked into my hand and saw a black guitar pick with a silver, glittery crucifix painted on its side.

At this point, another busker who had been watching us from the safety of a few blocks walked over. "Hey old man," he said to the drunk cowboy.

"What do you want?"

"Was wondering if you wanted to go get a drink with me," he said to the grizzled drunk.

"Okay."

They started walking away. The busker turned around after a few steps and said, "On a side note, buddy, you are playing in my spot, and if you know what's best, you'll vacate

A-S-A-P."

Then they disappeared into the nearest bar. I closed the guitar case and wandered to my van, put the seat back, and closed my eyes.

I had that bad dream again. There was a big electric cowboy picking up buses like toys, singing karaoke with Jesus' voice and telling me I'd burn on a cross for sins I never pulled off in Nashville. When I woke up, I was driving toward Memphis.

Downtown Alton, Indiana, is a big square. There is a government building in the center, and the downtown businesses live across the street on the outer edge of the square. It has a distinct, old-western-movie-set feel, and I was feeling like Clint Eastwood armed with a six string instead of a six shooter.

I parked in front of a saloon on an edge of the square at about seven o'clock that night. While I sat in the front seat trying to make up my mind about how to proceed, a big, muddy truck pulled up next to me. The driver was an older fellow, and he was finishing what appeared to be a joint. He parked the truck, took a last long puff, and looked out his window only to see me in the minivan, watching him. He started his truck again, backed out, and re-parked it about six spots away. Then he walked into the saloon.

I grabbed my guitar and entered soon after. Turns out the pickup driver was just starting his shift tending bar.

Setting my guitar case down and leaning on it, I introduced myself loudly enough for everyone in the bar to hear. "Hi. My name is D.B. Rouse, and I'm a musician from Wisconsin on my way to Seattle. Been playing music in every bar and diner along the way to cover gas. Was wondering if I could open my case and play here for a little while; maybe sell some CDs?"

Seven times out of ten, the answer was no. It was no for various reasons: the manager wasn't in, they didn't like the look of me, or didn't like music. About thirty percent of the time though...

"Yeah. Sure. Let's see what you got," the bartender replied with a stony-eyed, double-dog-dare grin.

I picked a spot by the door of the dim bar, put my guitar on, and left the case open on the floor. It had a sign taped to the inside lid saying: "Wisconsin musician en route to Seattle via Nashville. Tips for gas appreciated."

My first song was Roger Miller's 'King of the Road' and by the end, everyone in the bar was singing along. Forty-five minutes of music later and I was sitting at the bar, drinking my fourth beer and eating a greasy pub burger, all on the house.

I sat on a stool between a guy in a tie-dye shirt and an older, blonde lady going slightly gray. The tie-dyed fellow was keeping me company through my meal. "You sound great man. And as far as beggars go, you're a good one," he said.

"I don't really consider myself a beggar," I tried to say through a mouthful of burger.

"Exactly, man. That's just what I mean. A bum just sits and asks for money. You're a bum that provides a service. You earn your money."

"I prefer to be called a hobo, though technically, I'm a tire tramp."

"Well whatever you are, I'll gladly buy one of your little albums. I'll buy your next beer too," he said.

He got up and went into the bathroom, and I pondered while stuffing my face full of fries. It wasn't just the music that I was selling to the people; it was the story too.

Earlier that day I had stopped at a cafe in Green Castle, Indiana. I gave my sales pitch to the waitresses and people eating there, and they ran back to ask the manager if I could play. He wouldn't allow it, but one of the customers still ended up buying me a meal. Then another customer gave me a twenty spot for an album. It was like I had walked into a vicious generosity contest. I left that diner after a free meal, twenty dollars richer, without having played a single note on my Meal-ticket. The story and presentation sells as much, if not more than the music.

"Why Seattle?" the older lady next to me asked. She was dressed in what I guessed was her Sunday best, and smelled like she had been sneaking wine since church.

"I'm thinking about moving there. But I wanted to see the city first. Get to know it, you know? I got some friends waiting for me there," I said, downing the last of my beer.

"I just moved here mys-, myself," she sort of slurred at me. "Didn't get the chance to see this small town first, so I'm soaking it in now."

"Seems like a nice place," I said as she motioned the bartender for her seventh or eighth martini.

"We'll see," she said a little darkly. "I'm throwing a party to meet the neighbors next week. If you stick around, I'll hire you to play. My granddaughters will be visiting too."

"I'll be long gone by then," I said as the bartender plopped another martini in front of her.

She picked up her glass, looked into the alcohol, and said rather loudly, "These martinis are awful." This drew quizzical looks from the bartender and regulars, but they quickly went back to socializing and let it slide.

She set the glass down and said quietly to me, "These martinis are horrible. That's par for this course though. I lost a lot of money today, and I just found out I'm pregnant again."

My jaw dropped as she threw back the martini. I didn't know what to say or do, so I just turned and looked straight ahead at my reflection in the bar mirror for a few minutes. She started chatting with the regulars on her other side. What the hell was I doing there?

The tie-dye guy came back and sat next to me. "You all right?" he asked.

I nodded silently.

"Boy, looks like you could use a beer," he said, trying to get the tender's attention.

The bartender was a little preoccupied at that moment though. My drunken, pregnant grandmother friend had decided to get to know the locals by picking a fight.

"I think you've had enough, lady," the old bartender said, leaning toward her with a creased, pockmarked poker face.

His bleary eyes had become a cold, clear gray. "I know we've had enough of you."

The whole bar had grown quiet and was staring at the drama unfolding on center stage.

"I'm an adult. I can decide when I've had enough on my own. And this bar is open to everyone. If you let those asses drink here, so can I," she said pointing at a few of the regulars next to her.

"Am I going to have to escort you out?" the bartender asked rolling up his sleeves.

"No. I can escort myself. I was just about to leave this dumpster anyway." She fished her keys out of a sequined purse, and half stumbled on high heels out the door to her car. Then that drunk, pregnant grandmother drove away, and there was nothing to be done.

I played a few more songs, but the whole time the phrase 'Cut and run' was echoing in my head like a mantra. So when the tie-dye guy offered me a couch for the night, I said, "No thanks. I should get a few more miles in tonight."

This was the beginning of a lifelong problem that I would later refer to as 'Get out of Dodge Syndrome.' My attitude at that point was 'Get in, play music, get paid, and get out before something bad happens.' Whether or not I was picking up bad vibes, I always wanted to get out quick. It was one of the costs that I was paying for the illusion of security.

I feared that if I said too much or stayed too long, I would be found out for the con that I am. Everyone is a con artist to a certain degree. It's part of becoming an adult. But I felt then like I was blatantly crossing into swindler territory.

I started seeing visions of my guitar in flames, and me hanging from a tree while an angry mob shouted things like "You're not a real hobo!" and "You're a mediocre musician!"

So I grabbed all the money from my tips and album sales out of the guitar case, and stuffed it into my pockets. I never count money in front of the audience. I prefer to drive away like a bandit - pockets stuffed with cash, belly full of the spoils - and count it at my next stop.

My next stop was a rest area on a nearby interstate. It was

a cold end to a cold day, but I had ninety-one dollars of cold
hard cash in my pockets to keep me warm.

Highway 12 runs through my old college town. It's called Clairemont Avenue there. I remember stumbling down it as an underage drunk, headed to a hospital with a broken nose and blood gushing all over my shirt.

My college experience was in many ways a blinding flurry of parties. The old gang and I simply could not go far enough. We figured we had a mainline into the American dream, which for us was to get away with anything and everything we wanted.

Of course that all crashed and burned eventually. On that particular bloody night, a good friend of mine had punched me in the nose. He had cracked it and pushed it sidewise. I don't blame him though. I was sort of asking for it... literally.

We were well into a handle of tequila that night, and the subject of black eyes came up. I had never had one before, and I turned to my best drinking buddy and said, "You know what? I've never had a black eye before, but if I ever got one, I'd want it from you."

Connecting the dots from there is as easy as connecting a fist to a face.

Now, only a few years after I'd gotten out of school, I found myself back on good old Highway 12. The diploma - proof of the time I served there - was actually safety-pinned to the ceiling of the van.

Maybe it was to try and make amends with the turbulence that took place in my life on and around Highway 12, or maybe it was because the atlas was buried beneath a bag of clothes and a box of canned goods somewhere in the nether regions of the van, but I decided to ride it out; to take Highway 12 all the way to its end point in the West. It seemed far enough north that it would probably take me near Seattle. Besides, staying on 12 seemed a lot easier than digging the atlas out.

Through a large portion of Minnesota and South Dakota, Highway 12 unwinds right beside the old Burlington Northern Santa Fe railroad. I had been admiring and racing trains along the way. The minivan was a contender. We howled and blared banjo music as we raced.

I had just crossed into South Dakota, mid-train race, when I heard a tearing sound, and saw something that looked like a giant albino bat flutter out the open passenger-side window. It was my diploma. I grudgingly quit the race, and pulled off to the side of the road. The search for my education began.

This albino bat was the culmination of four-and-a-half years of my life. It represented four-and-a half drunken years of hungover classes - classes that prepared me for a system that no longer existed. I continued walking down Highway 12 towards the past.

Maybe I wasn't ready for college when I went. I didn't know what I wanted to do or be, and going to college was just what people did after high school, so I did it too. Because of this, all I really gained from the little albino blood-sucker was debt. Debt and an ability to con the system to a certain degree. I guess I should be thankful for that.

I found the bat. It was a little frazzled and torn, but no worse for the wear. It was flopping in the weeds on the shoulder of the road. I picked it up, but couldn't take it back to the van with me. I lifted it above my head, and waited for the right gust of wind to come. It flew off into the wild as the trains roared past into the sunset.

Happy hour is a profitable hour, and I was looking for a

place to play that evening. The first bar I walked into was in Big Stone Lake, South Dakota. I gave my pitch and started playing.

An old man was wiggling happily in his stool in front of a video gambling machine as its lights flashed, and he printed out a winning ticket. He decided to make it a good day for me as well. When I hit the right songs, he tipped me heavily. He was a shriveled old king atop a bar stool, basking in the glow of video poker. Eighty dollars later and I was headed back down the highway.

Things don't always come that easy on the road, so when it does happen you really need to make a point of enjoying it. This one jackpot of a stop would probably have to hold me through two or three days of bad stops and wrong turns; those days when no bar or diner will have you, or worse, when they do let you play, but you still can't raise a dime.

With eighty bucks burning a hole in my money box (stashed beneath the driver's seat), I decided to splurge and get a fancy place where I could stretch out my lanky legs and sleep. I pulled into the parking lot of a dilapidated building that looked like a tin storage facility. The 'O' was flashing in it's motel sign, but the thirty dollars sign shone loud and clear to me. I paid with a wad of cash, so the clerk was kind enough not to charge me tax.

I asked him, "Are there any good bars or diners nearby where a traveling musician might be able to make a quick buck?"

"Well there's the VFW in town. Otherwise, there's a strip club about fifteen miles down the road. That place is usually packed. The strippers would probably still expect you to tip them, even if you're playing, but you could make a little money there."

I tried to picture a stripper pole-dancing to acoustic Bob Dylan covers. It was a pleasant picture, but also somewhat awkward.

"Thanks for the tip," I said.

After lounging in the deteriorating, coffee-stain colored motel room for a while, I found myself in a battle with road weariness. I didn't feel much like playing anymore; just wanted a beer. But you never know when your ship is coming in, so I still grabbed my guitar for the couple-block walk to the VFW.

The VFW had only six people in it. 'No reason to push myself here,' I thought. So I leaned Meal-ticket against the wooden bar, took a stool and ordered a beer. I told some of my story to the friendly tender who was curious about the guitar. After drinking two thirds of the bottle, a very intoxicated forty-something lady approached me.

"Can I play your guitar?" she asked. She seemed far too drunk to handle my Meal-ticket, but I could also see by the look on her face that there would be no reasoning with her. A diversion needed to be made.

"How 'bout if I play you a song?" I offered.

"Okay, guitar boy."

Then she called the attention of her man and friends at the other end of the bar. "Hey! Hey! Shut up, you little shits! Guitar boy here is going to play us a song."

I chose a spot in the center of the bar and opened the guitar case on the table next to me for tips. As I tuned and readied Meal-ticket, they grew impatient.

"You gonna play or what?" asked the drunk lady's man in a slightly more aggressive tone than I liked.

"You folks know Otis Redding?" I asked. This question was greeted with staring silence. "All right then," I went on, "let's find out."

I started in on 'Dock of the Bay' and was relieved to see the weird tension break as they ordered another round of beer. Every once in a while I'd take requests and they'd tip a little. I had been playing for the small crowd for about half an hour, and had just started CCR's 'Bad Moon Rising' when the drunk lady climbed up on top of the bar and dragged her tube-topped, barefooted sister behind her. That would have been fine except they were so drunk that they were having trouble walking, let alone dancing on a bar. There was indeed a bad moon on the rise.

While singing, I tried to give the bartender a look that said

'Are you actually going to let this happen?'

Instead, the tender read my look as saying, 'Hey this is fun and smart. You should clap and encourage them.'

The barefooted sister fell first. She bumped her head on a light and slipped on a spilled drink. The other one got dragged down when she tried to catch the first. They fell in slow motion, hair flying, a tangle of legs and skin and tube tops in the dim neon lights. Chairs broke. Tables fell over. The music stopped, but the blood never flowed.

The bartender and husbands dashed over with worried looks on their faces. The ladies were both surprisingly in one piece, though a little bruised perhaps, especially in the ego department. One of the husbands reached out to help them up, but they refused.

"We're just going to sit on the floor for a minute and gather our bearings."

The other husband was thoughtful enough to bring their drinks over to them so the ladies could nurse their wounds on the floor.

After seeing that they were all right, and checking bar time, I decided it was time to get out of Dodge. I closed the night with a special rendition of Tom Petty's 'Free Fallin" which the husbands loved; the women on the floor… not so much.

I shut the guitar case and made my way back to the crumbling motel where I spent the majority of the rest of the night paranoid about bedbugs, and scratching at invisible worries.

I continued Highway 12 that morning. It was starting to have a cozy, homey feeling to it. I drove through the southwest corner of North Dakota and into the great wide nothings of Eastern Montana. There was the highway, the big old blue sky, the van, and nothing else. I drove into the nothing, and the nothing swallowed me. I became nothing.

In a way, driving through this section of Montana was like driving back in time. Each tiny town that did pop up had a gravel ditch that served as Main Street, and maybe a gas station that doubled as a grocery store that tripled as a post office.

After driving a lifetime, I hit a mountain range called the Crazy Mountains. That name made sense. I was getting cabin fever and going a little stir crazy. Relief came soon after the mountains as the DeLorean and I came across some towns from my time, like White Sulphur Springs.

I parked on the main drag in White Sulphur Springs, grabbed Meal-ticket, and walked past a large biker gang lounging about in a little green space on my way to the nearest bar. I asked the nervous, clean-cut bartender if I could play, and I could tell by his shifty, untrusting demeanor and the small amount of patrons at the bar that my odds were not likely.

Before he could answer me though, a large, gray-haired biker wearing a bandanna and sunglasses who had been sipping on water and watching us from the other end of the bar walked over and asked me, "Are ya going to play guitah here?" He had a thick German accent.

"I'm not sure yet," I answered while slowly looking to the bartender, "but I hope so."

The biker got my drift, and without missing a beat he turned to the bartender and said, "If he plays here, I vill bring all de bikahs with me in here to eat suppa, ya? About twenty-five of us. Ve'ah hungry."

The bartender looked at me. "Well I guess you're playing."

"Ve all flew in to Seattle from Germany," the gray-haired biker explained to me. "Ve'ah on our vay to Sturgis for de annual rally." He walked outside to round up his gang.

Meanwhile, the bartender and waitress had started preparing a separate dining room for us. There were two large, rectangular tables with red-and-white-checkered tablecloths underneath chandeliers made of elk antlers. The bikers came in the back door, one by one, chattering away in German. They were mostly men, but some women too. Their ages ranged between twenty and fifty. They certainly dressed the part of leather-clad bikers, but there was something polished about them. You could tell it was a hobby, not a lifestyle.

I was tuned up and ready by the time they were all seated. I hit my first chord and let it ring. It hung in the air like smoke and attracted everyone's attention. They were oddly quiet. I started playing 'Folsom Prison Blues' and the song was the only sound in the bar. I couldn't remember having ever captivated an audience that way with a Johnny Cash cover. When it was over, they applauded enthusiastically. I gave a little bow and went into the next tune. Twenty minutes went by without a tip. They were all well into their meals by then, and it didn't make sense to me. Were they all just going to tip at the end? Did they think I was horrible? Then I remembered what I had heard about Europeans and tipping.

Salesman and con artist that I am, I decided that maybe a little persuasion was in order. "Now I know you are all from Germany, and that not all Europeans are familiar with the tipping traditions here. But I'm a traveling musician on my way to Seattle. I'm paying for all my gas by playing music and collecting tips…"

The majority of the bikers had stopped eating and sort of stared at me blankly. They didn't really know English. My eyes found the biker who had talked my way into playing there. He smiled at me and said, "I translate."

He explained my shameless speech in German for the rest of the bikers. It sounded somehow more delightful and ridiculous in German than when it first came out of my mouth. They reacted pleasantly to his translation; a few people got up to throw a handful of dollars into my case while sort of chuckling at me.

When I played 'Heart of Gold' it was like finding the right key on a giant keychain to open the crowd up. The bikers put down their forks and knives, wiped gravy from their beards, and sang every word with me. They barely knew any English, yet they all knew Neil Young by heart.

The currency started to flow a little quicker. One fellow tipped a five spot, and I explained as best I could that that was what I charged for CDs. I pulled one from a stack in my guitar case and handed it to him. Once they figured out I was selling albums, the money really came in. They seemed more willing to part with their money for physical objects than for simply listening to me play. The German biker gang bought every record I walked in with.

When they paid the bills and left, they left a happy bartender and a guitar player seventy-five dollars richer with no place but west to go.

I had a new game to play. I was going to stay at a motel in some city for a week to get the discounted weekly rate. I was then going to spend that week working the town to make back the motel money, and hopefully more. I chose to play this game in Missoula, Montana.

The cheapest motel I could find downtown was $230 per week. I checked in, paid with my tip money, and plopped into bed. Two days later I woke up, cased the downtown businesses, and poked around to see if any place would let me play.

Missoula is kind of a hub for transients and vagrants. This is probably one of the reasons why I was drawn to it, like a moth to a flame. But like a lot of the other places I've been drawn to, I must have been drawn too late. Missoula was already oversaturated with my traveling, unemployed brethren. I noticed them scattered throughout the downtown area, trying to hitch rides to exotic places scrawled on their cardboard signs. Wherever I went I found unshaven, greasy men begging on sidewalks with mangy dogs; lost soldiers in search of the big rock candy mountain. The townsfolk seemed thoroughly sick of us and all of our panhandling tricks. Every place I asked to play, I was met with a shake of the head and a request that I leave. No bar or cafe wanted anything to do with me unless I was spending money, no matter how fancy I dressed up. A hobo with a bowtie is still a hobo.

When it dawned on me that I might not be able to find any place to play in town, I didn't really know what to do. I had

230 dollars invested in this, and I was in danger of losing it all. So I grabbed a local paper and scanned it for open mics. There was only one listed. The whole experiment felt like a bust.

The one true lead I did find was a farmers market happening in town the next day. I hadn't played at a farmers market before, and thought I might as well give it a try.

I walked downtown in the early morning to a street that had been blocked off for the market. I walked past a man selling vegetables, a lady selling hand carved flutes, a man selling paintings, and a handful of various food and craft booths until I stumbled upon a nice centrally-located curb. On that curb I opened up my guitar case with that familiar gas money sign still clinging to the lid. I noticed that a nearby bald sunglasses vendor was paying very close attention to me. His arms were crossed as he looked me over, and I judge he was judging me.

It was sunny, and the people were generous. Because the venders dealt mostly in cash instead of cards, everyone there seemed to be carrying paper money, which makes it easier to tip musicians and the like.

At one point, a religious-hippy type walked up to me from his wood carving shanty. "This is for you," he said as he dropped a leather necklace with a hand-carved wooden crucifix into my case. Then a lady running a food cart came up and gave me a frozen chocolate -covered banana.

Four hours later I started packing up. The sunglasses vendor, bald head glowing in the sun, walked over to me. "You sounded real good," he said, and he shook my hand.

"Well thanks for putting up with my racket," I responded with a smile.

"This is my market," he went on. "I manage and run it. Usually I kick out musicians after a few songs, but you were good enough to keep around."

"Thanks for letting me stay," I said. I handed him a CD.

"Hey, I do some booking around here too. You got a number I could reach you at?"

"I'm only in town for a few days, but I would love to find another place to play." I wrote the number of the motel I was staying at on the back of the CD cover. The whole thing went off better than I had hoped.

That evening I stayed in my motel room and relaxed. I ate macaroni and cheese cooked in the room's microwave, watched a little TV and enjoyed all those little things I usually take for granted, like showering.

At some point I got a call. "Hey man, it's Sam from the market. I just finished listening to your CD, and I want to invite you out to a barbecue with my family tomorrow evening."

"Sure," I told him. "That sounds great. Should I bring anything?"

"Just bring that old guitar of yours and be prepared to sing for your supper."

I laughed and he filled me in on the rest of the details.

When I parked at Sam's house, the first thing I noticed was all of his toys. He had snowmobiles, dirt bikes, boats, and jet skis parked in various places about his yard and driveway.

Sam answered the door like an old friend and invited me in to meet the family. We had a feast of potatoes and ribs. Sam bragged to me about his two sons while they quietly ate next to me.

"They worked the wheat harvest for a couple seasons," he explained. "Went from Oklahoma through Canada driving combines. They made damn good money, boy."

Seasonal jobs had always interested me (at least as far as my interest in jobs go). Those are jobs that have the built-in security of not becoming permanent. They usually pay pretty well, and when the season is over, you can up and leave with your chunk of cash and start a whole new life.

"How'd you guys land that job?" I asked his sons.

"We knew some people... but you probably wouldn't want that job," one of them replied. "You drive the combine from daylight to daybreak, eat cheap food, and stay in crappy motel rooms. It's not really all that glamorous 'er nothing." He took a bite on his rib.

Then the other son started up. "It does get a little exciting with rain days. We'd go into the nearest town and spend all the money we earned on the first pretty girl we met."

"Well that sounds like the way I'm living now anyway," I said. "Except without the steady pay."

I watched Sam mow down his ribs with his wife acting like his waitress. He had an old-fashioned, kingly air about him; sort of exuded an attitude that said this was his kingdom and he was proud.

After dinner, they lit a campfire and I sang for a few hours. They tried their best to get me drunk and have me crash in their RV - another toy somewhere around the yard. I thanked them profusely, and kept just barely sober enough to drive back to the motel at about 2:30 AM. I gave Sam a few more albums before I left, and he slipped me a twenty spot for the road.

Behind the college in Missoula, there's a mountain with a giant letter 'M' made of whitewashed concrete about midway up the side. I decided to hike to it the next morning. Nothing works for a little hangover like hiking up a mountain.

When I got to the 'M' I decided to just keep going. After all, I was once an athlete. An hour later and I was at the top of the mountain where a lone woman was hula-hooping. You could see all of Missoula in the valley below.

"Hi, how are you?" I asked the hoop enthusiast.

"Okay. You?"

"Not bad."

A cloud of bugs had started to descend on me, but I also

saw a bluebird darting about.

"Missoula seems like a real nice town," I said while gazing into the valley.

"It is," she said. "But everyone I know is moving to Austin, Texas."

Austin: now there's one flame this moth hadn't flown into yet.

She turned around and started down the trail, rolling her hula hoop beside her. Maybe I should have rolled down with her, but I stayed to enjoy the view of Missoula for as long as the swarms of bugs would let me.

I went to busk later that night near Missoula's concert hall. Brandi Carlile was playing, and people were lined up for three blocks to get inside. They sort of became my captive audience; certainly not captivated, but captive nonetheless. That put sixty dollars into the case.

I tallied the points on my final night in Missoula and found I had lost the game. I made about $170 altogether that week. It may have been a financial bust, but I did enjoy myself. I got to rest, and most importantly I learned about farmer and craft markets.

The next morning meant Highway 12 again. It was strange to think that I could take the road straight back from Missoula and end up at my old stomping grounds in Wisconsin. Someone I knew was probably driving on the same road back there at that very moment. Nothing is really all that far away.

The miles added up. The odometer rolled over in its sleep as the terrain blew past my open window. Idaho was a breeze. I camped on a white sand beach alongside the crisp Lochsa River off the Lolo Pass. I didn't find a place to play, but I did get a free breakfast and sold a few albums to a religious zealot who was camping a few spots from my tent. He had heard me rehearsing and invited me over.

"Were you raised religious?" he asked me over eggs and coffee.

"Yup. I was raised Catholic."

"You poor thing. You're just a Mary-worshipping Pagan baby."

"What?" I said with a confused grin, thinking he was joking.

"In Catholicism people pray to saints and Mary just as much as God the Father, but all those saints and Mary are just false idols."

I held my tongue. I was eating his eggs and drinking his coffee, I could put up with almost anything for the duration of breakfast.

He had an SUV parked near the picnic table, and was blaring Christian Rock music out of it. I felt bad for the other campers around us. I felt bad for myself too.

"But at least you're not Islamic," he went on. "The Koran is truly the work of the Devil."

That's the strange thing about the human mind:

whether or not what you believe makes sense, if you believe anything hard enough, it will become real to you.

I made my exit down the lost highway to hell as soon as I could, but not before I had sold him some of my Godless music, and he forced a Bible on me with a CD of a Christian preacher, preaching hate in Jesus' name. I took all I could from him.

Fast forward through the desert of Eastern Washington and into the mountains. I stopped at some fruit stands in the Yakima Valley (where the majority of our apples come from), and bought some fresh cherries. I asked if they had any leads on seasonal orchard jobs, but everyone was very closed-mouthed about the orchards. I guess the government had recently cracked down on the valley for hiring a lot of illegal immigrants. That should have meant that there were apple picking jobs to be filled, but I couldn't get a straight answer from anyone.

I found a spooky campground in the mountains. It obviously hadn't been maintained for some time, unless of course they were going for that overgrown, un-mowed junkyard vibe. The old trees around it had the look of arthritic hands reaching out of a freshly-dug grave. I wouldn't have stayed there normally, but they had peacocks. A dozen of them were roaming freely through the campground. 'A campground with peacocks can't be bad,' I rationalized, so I checked in.

I curled up in my nest of a sleeping bag, and fell asleep soon after dark. Around 3 AM the wind started howling like a werewolf and woke me halfway up. The sound of a giant branch cracking off a tree and crashing to the ground woke me up entirely. The tent shuddered when the branch hit the ground.

I wanted to at least move my van out of harm's way, back up to the road where no tree would threaten to total it. Plans changed when I poked my head out of the tent and smelled the unmistakably strong odor of skunk. For some reason at that moment the thought of being sprayed by a skunk was scarier than gambling on my van's life in the tree cemetery. So like a turtle, I retreated into my shell of a tent. I felt cornered, and sure that the next limb would fall on either me or my van.

'So this is how it ends.' I took a deep breath, and tried to just accept it. 'But I can't die yet,' I remember thinking. 'I still have songs to write.'

The werewolves eventually wandered off, and I slept restlessly until daybreak. The sun rose to a soundtrack of peacocks. They are really just extravagant roosters after all. They sounded like crazed trumpet players - like Dizzy Gillespie in drag.

I took a shower before I hit the dusty highway. I smelled worse than skunk, I smelled like fear. I saw a frog in the shower, and it went ahead and showered with me. I was awkwardly one with nature.

The van led the way through the misty mountains, past Mt. Rainer. When I did finally start paying attention to the road signs, I noticed that Seattle wasn't very far away. Highway 12 had a junction with I-5 and I merged onto it, leaving my little old highway behind. It seemed only logical to take the direct route to my destination. I was so close now. Had I taken Highway 12 to its end, I would have gone miles in the wrong direction.

I was speeding down one of those newfangled interstates to what I hoped was going to be my new base camp. I looked at the gas stations, fast food restaurants, and hotel chains that lined the freeway. I was back in the thick of Interstate Culture. I could have been on any interstate in the country, and it would look just like this one.

I was about ten miles removed from my little highway when I finally couldn't take it anymore. Highway 12 wasn't going in the wrong direction, because there was no wrong direction for me to go in. Wasn't it that wise old Cheshire Cat that once said, "When you don't know where you're going, any road will take you there."

I turned the van around. I had come this far on 12; I needed to finish it. I pictured the highway ending at a beach on the Pacific. I pictured myself lounging on the hood of the van, eating a victory peanut butter and honey sandwich while seagulls circled overhead and waves lapped against the beach. I did not picture Highway 12 petering out in the middle of an industrial lumber town.

The welcome sign read: "Welcome to Aberdeen: Come as you are." I thought it strange that they would use Nirvana lyrics for the motto, until I read on the sign underneath that this was Kurt Cobain's hometown.

Highway 12 came to an end in the heart of Aberdeen's little downtown, which from the looks of the worn out and abandoned store fronts was just barely limping its way through the recession. I parked the van next to a bank, and took a picture of the sign that said: "HWY 12- END."

I was happy at first. I was a conqueror, and had finished another conquest. I beat Highway 12. This feeling was quickly overshadowed with a hint of, 'Well, what now?' Raise some money to get to Seattle was what.

There were a couple of unhappy hours left in the afternoon, so I wandered into a coffee house with a book. I mentioned to the barista that I was a musician and she immediately showered me with questions.

"What kind of music do you play?" she asked.

"What kind do you listen to?" I answered.

"A little bit of everything."

"I play that."

She rolled her eyes. "Where are you from?"

"Wisconsin."

"If you're going to be here a while, we could set up a show for you here."

Because of Kurt Cobain, music was of course a big deal here. I don't think the town was big enough to really even have a music scene, but that wasn't for lack of trying. It was here that Kurt Cobain rose from the ashes of poverty on the wings of music, and in doing so he gave hope to everyone in the community. Then he went and offed himself.

"I'll be leaving soon, I think. But thanks. I'll be sure to drop by if I'm ever in town again." I gave the barista a CD on my way out.

The bar I found to play in was on the industrial side of town. It was an older bar made out of the large logs that have been the foundation of Aberdeen's economy. As I was setting up, one of the barflies mentioned that Kurt had grown up only a few blocks from that bar, and probably even got drunk in there once or twice.

I felt as though experiencing Aberdeen somehow caused Nirvana's music to make a little more sense to me. I didn't play any Nirvana covers that night. Instead I played old-time country music Kurt Cobain probably hated.

Seattle.

My old friend Zak had a place there so I gave him a call.
Sure enough, the number he had given me years ago was real
and still worked. He and his girlfriend, Ella, had a basement
apartment in the Green Lake neighborhood. They opened the
door to me, and I made myself at home on their couch. Then
I promptly started planning my coup of the Seattle Farmers
Market Alliance.

The plan wasn't exactly complicated. I showed up at the
farmers market the next day and asked the manager about
playing there. As planned, he said I could, but since they already had scheduled music at a 'Featured Musician Tent' I
would have to play on the opposite side of the market. To
the dismay of the featured musicians, my plan was working.
I set up shop and moved in for the kill. I may not have won
their hearts, but I did win handfuls of fresh lettuce, tomatoes,
potatoes, onions, and cash.

The Seattle Farmers Market Alliance ran a different market in a different Seattle neighborhood each day of the week.
So I showed up at the next neighborhood the following day.
I went to every neighborhood they went to, and before long
they had gotten familiar with me. By the end of the first week,

I became the featured musician with the glamorous tent.

It was a nice deal. I made out like an organic bandit; fistfuls of money and I was able to pay my daily rent on the couch with the produce. Relations with my friends/'couch lords' were going great. We were catching up every night over fresh food dinners. If I didn't know any better, I'd say that Zak and Ella almost liked having me around. But I do know better.

Zak was a muscular fellow I had known through a friend back in Wisconsin. He used to be a rowdy one, but a couple years and Ella seemed to have mellowed him out a bit. Now he was going back to school in Seattle to study environmentalism and green ways of producing energy. So it came as little surprise to me when he said one evening, "Have you ever heard of freeganism?"

"You mean dumpster diving?"

"Well dumpster diving with a twist of philosophy. It's making a statement about American consumerism and waste."

"Or is it really just a way to try and justify taking food out of the garbage?" I asked

"Either way man, why let perfectly good - or just slightly bad - food go to waste?"

"I'm certainly not above it. Let's do it."

The very next day, after a stint at the market, Zak drove me past tin-can warehouses on the industrial side of town where the Naked Health Juice Company was located.

We parked alongside a giant dumpster protected by a shoulder-height chain link fence.

"How do we do this?" I asked him.

"I'll climb the fence and throw juice over to you," Zak said.

"Okay. Should we keep the car running?" I asked.

"That's not a bad idea," he said. We stared at the dumpster and glanced around to see if anyone was watching.

"Let's do it," Zak said and darted out of the car with me following, leaving the doors open.

Zak shimmied up and over the fence, and then climbed into the dumpster. "Eureka, I have found it!" he shouted.

There was literally hundreds of dollars' worth of barely-expired juice in there. Zak piled bottles into some cardboard boxes that were lying on the pavement. He handed them over the fence, and I toted them back to his car. We took four or five dozen bottles in all, and sped back to Zak's house to fill his fridge up with all the healthy goodness. All those bottles looked beautiful in the cool glow of the refrigerator light. We couldn't stop laughing as we chugged so much juice and felt so healthy that we both almost vomited.

To work off our health juice binge, we decided to bike to a brewery and down a couple cold ones.

"I got an extra bike you can ride, it'll be fun. It's a good way to cap off a healthy day full of fresh vegetables and old juice," Zak said.

"I don't know. It's been a while since I've ridden a bike."

"It's really easy. It's like riding a bike."

"All right, all right."

It wasn't until about ten miles in that I really started to question him. "Where is this place?"

"We're not far now, man."

"That's what you said ten minutes ago. I'm starting to hurt."

"Buck up."

We eventually got there after mile eighteen. "This better be good," I mumbled to Zak as we walked inside.

And of course it was good. It was a brewery. It was so good in fact, that for a little while I completely forgot about the impending eighteen-mile bike ride back. Forgetting doesn't make anything go away though. Don't forget that.

Maybe I should have hung my hat on the Space Needle and called Seattle home. But due to lack of real employment, general homelessness, and a feeling that two weeks was the maximum amount of time I could spend on Zak's couch without becoming a major nuisance, I started driving again. I was too busy having fun to figure out that other nonsense.

I still wonder what my life would have been like had I set up camp there. I don't know whether or not leaving was a bad choice, but I do know for a fact that I've made an awful lot of bad choices since - bad choices I would not have had the opportunity to make had I stuck around that area. Then again, I'm sure staying in Seattle would have come with its own barrage of bad choices.

The first bad choice I had to make was 'Where next?' The two options I was toying with were Portland and a Jesuit Monastery south of Portland. I had heard that the monastery was offering three months room and board in exchange for work and a vow of silence. Since Portland was on the way to the monastery, I thought I should at least stop into the city and figure things out from there. Some don't like flying by the seat of their pants. For others, it is a way of life.

Portland is not what I would call user-friendly. I ended up taking a bad turn... several bad turns. I found myself in Portland suburbia, being cut off by local traffic left and right. I had a rare flash of road rage. I wanted to take all those winding roads, strangle them together like neckties, put them into a bigger knot than they were already in, and throw them into the Pacific Ocean. Then I'd mount some machetes onto the hood of the van, and blaze my own trail.

By the time I stopped seeing red and got my bearings, I was well outside of Portland, heading away from the monastery, and back towards the coast.

"Fine, pants seat," I said to my jeans. "This is the direction you want to take us, then let's go."

I noticed while chatting with my pants that they were getting worn out. My jeans appeared to be on their last legs. I also noticed that I was talking to my jeans, which started me questioning myself.

Much like my jeans, I was getting worn out. The general road weariness was building, and I could see my safe haven state of Wisconsin in the not-so-distant future.

Seaside, Oregon.

I was busking again. The street I set up on was filled with tourist shops and hotels, milling with people in bright T-shirts and shorts. At the end of the street was a statue of Louis and Clark with the limitless backdrop of the Pacific Ocean behind it. I had only been playing for about twenty-five minutes but already raised thirty-odd dollars from the friendly crowds. I noticed a cop noticing me and my small audience. After I finished 'Stand by Me' he tried to get my attention. I started playing 'All You Need is Love' instead of heeding him.

"Excuse me! There's a town ordinance. You can't play here," he half-shouted at me. He had a little mustache and a big gun, and looked like just about every police officer that has stopped someone from playing music in the streets of America.

I stopped playing as he got right up in front of me. "Can I see some ID?"

I started fishing in my pocket for my wallet, while a little six or seven-year-old boy who had stopped to hear 'All You Need is Love' flipped the cop off behind his back. Suppressing giggles, I took out my license and handed it over to him.

"Where are you staying?" he asked me severely.

"Oh, I'm just passing through," I answered as care-freely as I could.

He studied my faded Wisconsin license. "Good. But where are you staying tonight?"

"Maybe I'll camp somewhere. I'm not actually sure at the moment. I'll figure all that later."

He tapped my ID in his other hand and looked me directly in the eyes. "What are you, some kind of vagrant?"

"Well... no, I wouldn't say vagrant really."

"Why are you in Seaside? Family? Friends?"

"No family here. No friends here yet. I just stopped to make some music, make some money, and then spend it all at your fine bars."

I stopped short of saying, "And to buy cigarettes for all these friendly youngsters running around." Through an experience I had at the Canadian Border - and the experience I was to eventually have at the Mexican border - I was already in the process of realization that the law does not have a sense of humor.

"You driving a vehicle?" he asked.

"Yes sir."

He handed my license back. "I want you to drive away from Seaside, and I don't want you to come back. If I find you here in Seaside again, you won't be able to drive away. We'll impound your vehicle and put you in the tank for vagrancy."

He turned around and walked back towards his parked squad car.

"Hey! Can I at least finish the song I was playing when you interrupted me?" What I wouldn't have given to have known NWA's 'F tha Police' on acoustic guitar right then.

He turned, glared at me and shook his head no, so I took a bow and left Seaside.

Busker

SWIMMING IN IT

My memory gets hazy here. I drove through the Redwoods in Northern California. It was like weaving through a herd of Brontosaurus legs. I remember lying on the roof of the van and looking up in awe at those ancient giants, convinced that they were holding the sky up.

I remember playing a farmers market in Stockton, California. As the market was ending, a Mafioso-type manager complete with gold chains and a track suit cussed me out for having been there without his permission. I tried to ignore him and drown him out by playing louder whenever he talked to me. He eyed the thirty dollars I had gathered in my case as though he was going to try and take a cut of it. Instead, he told me to leave and not come back.

I don't remember leaving, but I do remember the distinct feeling that it was all too much for me to really absorb anymore. My head was full up.

I started burning the midnight motor oil, planning to make as quick of a burn back to Wisconsin as possible - back to the safety of old friends and family. There I would have a chance to digest everything that had and hadn't happened. Wisconsin was pulling at my van like a giant magnet.

I made a stop at a little oil town in Wyoming and worked two different bars on the same street. The first crowd was composed mostly of sophisticated rednecks who had drilled liquid money out of their front yards. For them I played a forty-five minute set of country and western music. Almost one hundred dollars later, and I was walking down the street to the second bar.

This bar was actually a microbrewery. It was built in an old Sears building, and had great acoustics. Beatles and Stones posters littered the walls, and the patrons were mostly twenty-somethings. I was well into a classic rock set when my eyes fell on her.

All of a sudden my road weariness washed away like dirt down the shower drain. The fuzzy edges I had been seeing on everything sharpened up. She had long legs, and was wearing short khaki shorts and a tank top. She had long, dark brown hair. I watched her step up to the bar and down a shot like a champ. Then she turned to me, with her back slightly arched, and she stared at me with stunning green eyes through a little too much eyeliner. She put her hands on her hips and squinted those emerald eyes at me as though I had done something wrong.

And I had actually done something wrong. I got lost while staring at her, and 'Here Comes the Sun' had suffered a handful of missed chords. I stopped the song abruptly, gave a goofy smile, and broke into the Stones' 'Honky Tonk Women.' They give me the honky-tonk blues. I saw her start singing along before I finally forced my eyes off of her. I felt awake, and I finished the classic rock set with an energy and gusto I hadn't felt since Indiana.

Sitting down at the bar afterwards, enjoying a free beer and burger, I was planning on getting out of there as soon as I could. I wanted to chat up Emerald Eyes, but I didn't want trouble, and she looked like trouble.

Trouble found me, and took a seat on the next stool. Then she scooted that stool right beside me so we were almost touching. She was staring at me, just piercing me; impaling me on her green eyes. I put my burger down and looked at her with as much of a standoff vibe as I could muster, but I felt it melt into a sheepish grin.

"Yes?" I asked.

"You sounded okay up there tonight. I liked your song choices."

"Thanks," I said and turned my attention back to my burger.

"I couldn't help but notice," she went on, "that the sign in your guitar case says you're going to Wisconsin."

"Yup, I'm headed back. I was going to move to Nashville but it didn't really seem like my kind of town. Then I was going to move to Seattle, but that didn't really pan out either. I guess I don't really know what I'm doing anymore."

"That's funny," she said. " 'Cos I'm going back to Wisconsin too."

"Really? Where in Wisconsin?"

"I'm going back to college in La Crosse."

"Ohhh, I know La Crosse. La Crosse is fun. I went to school in Eau Claire, not far from there."

"You still studying there?" she asked.

"No. I graduated eventually, with a degree in Philosophy, which is why you see me here today."

"You just going back to visit family then?"

"Yup," I said. "Going to visit family and recuperate in Wisconsin for a while... figure out my next move. Maybe find some seasonal work somewhere."

She put her hand on my arm and leaned in towards me. "You driving back there all by yourself?"

I looked at her long fingers on my arm, her neckline, and her face. She was pouting her not-quite plump lips. It occurred to me how hard she was trying to be sexy. It was ridiculous, yet somehow endearing. Truth be told, she didn't need to try.

"Yup."

"Must get awful lonesome out there, all by yourself."

"Well it's like Townes Van Zandt once said," I spoke, trying to sound poetic and suave. "There's a difference between loneliness and being alone."

"I don't suppose you'd have room for one more? I just gotta get back soon for school."

"Well..." I took a bite of my burger and chewed it thoughtfully, and looked at her pouting lips. "Why should I trust you?"

She ordered a couple more shots of whiskey from the bartender. "Listen, I just need a ride back to Wisconsin. I promise no silly business. I can help drive, and I can chip in for gas. I can even help sing a little at your next stop. If you say no, it's all right. I'll just find myself another ride, no sweat off my back."

"Are you in some kind of trouble with the laws or something?" I asked.

"No. Are you?"

"No. But why are you here in Wyoming?"

"I have a boyfriend out here. Well, I had one. We're breaking up; he just doesn't know it yet."

The bartender dropped the whiskey shots in front of us. She held up her shot glass towards me and asked, "Well, what do you say?"

I picked mine up, and looked into it like it was a Magic Eight Ball toy that had the answer floating there. "I say we leave very soon."

We touched glasses and downed the shots. She coughed

and gave me a big smile. "By the way, my name is Lauren."

"Nice to meet you Lauren, I'm D.B."

She was a professional drinker. Nothing really seemed to affect her. She ordered another round of shots... then another... and another. I vaguely remember that it started raining at some point in the night. Then it hailed.

I regained my auditory senses first. I heard the van moving along the highway. I heard the windshield wipers slapping time to Kris Kristofferson's 'Me and Bobby McGee' on the radio. For a second or two, everything seemed normal and right in the world. Then I felt my head throbbing, and realized that I wasn't even driving the van. I remembered having met Lauren as if it happened in a dream. My eyes jolted open.

She was driving my van, wearing sunglasses and the clothes I had met her in the previous night. I was soaking wet and sprawled out awkwardly across the passenger seat.

"This is actually happening?" I asked her in a rough voice that surprised me.

She turned and gave me a warm smile. "This is happening," she said matter-of-factly. "I just can't believe everything that happened last night."

"What - what all happened last night? Why are you driving my van? Where are we going?"

"You really can't hold your drink, can you?" she said almost laughing. Was she enjoying this? The sadist. "There's a bottle of water by your feet, you might want to drink some," she pointed out.

"I guess I'm a little out of practice when it comes to drinking," I said reaching for the half-empty bottle. "Or maybe I'm just not an alcoholic like you. What the hell is going on? What happened last night, Lauren?" I paused trying to remember, "Lauren is your name, right?"

"It sure is, Ben."

I had apparently told her that the 'B' in D.B. stands for Ben. I know D.B. is kind of a pretentious-sounding name, so I tell my friends to call me Ben. That must mean that we became friends at some point in the night.

"Well Ben, after a few shots and a long discussion about music at the bar, you and I took the place over and did some duets together."

"Duets? I don't duet. I work alone."

"Not last night. We tore the house down doing a Dylan and Sublime medley. We raised about fifty more dollars. I'm putting my half towards gas."

"Okay... so I take it we're driving towards Wisconsin at the moment?" It felt like there was a heart shaped like a mallet pounding at the inside of my skull.

"Wisconsin, yup. We needed to leave quick," she said.

"Oh? Why's that?"

"We dropped by my ex-boyfriend's house to pick up my bag and my banjo."

"Banjo?"

"Yes sir. Jake did not take kindly to this new turn of events. He almost got physical with me, until you stepped up and kicked him in the balls. Kind of a cheap shot, but I'll take it. Jake more or less ran us out of town with a baseball bat after that."

"What the hell are you talking about? I feel like I would remember something like that."

"Well I was feeding you drinks all night, honey. You were mighty thirsty."

"I thought you said no funny business..." I started but couldn't finish.

"I did. And you probably don't remember, but you got a little overly amorous with me last night, boy. I slapped you a good one. You kept talking about Bonnie and Clyde and getting out of Dodge." She paused, and I drank in her silence. "Ben?"

"Huh?" My head was going to explode right there, and my biggest concern was that the van would soon be stained with my blood.

"I just want a ride to Wisconsin. I'm not looking for a relationship."

"Good. That makes two of us," I tried to fire back. Then I felt it coming. "Pull over," I gasped.

"What?"

"Pull over! Pull OVER!"

She pulled off the side of the highway. Then I opened up my window and let it all out. The vomit burned my throat and my nostrils but it felt good to release it. Out of fear that Lauren might drive off without me, I stayed in the van and just leaned my head out the window and spewed a river into the rain.

"Christ, Ben," I heard Lauren say.

Lauren was studying geology at college, and for geological or geographical purposes, she decided we should camp at Yellowstone. That was fine by me. I needed to get out of the car and get some fresh air. We pulled into camp at about 1 PM in the soggy afternoon and set up my raggedy tent in silence. I was still feeling ill when I wandered off to the camp bathrooms to take a shower and wash the vomit out of my hair. By this time, I was confident that Lauren wasn't going to take off in the van with all of my worldly possessions. She could have done that at any point the night before, but didn't. It was actually almost insulting if I thought about it too hard.

When I got back, she was sitting on top of the damp picnic table, plucking away on her banjo and humming.

I walked past her to crawl into the tent. "Great," I said. "Surely your banjo will help this hangover."

She stopped playing and asked, "Are you always this sour?"

I was wiggling into my sleeping bag cocoon when I heard her pop open the case to put her instrument away.

"Wait," I said through the open tent door flap. "I'm sorry. Actually, I'd like to hear you play."

She gazed at me. Her dark hair was pulled back and she looked like one of the undocumented geological wonders of Yellowstone. She took the banjo back out and took her seat on top of the picnic table, facing me with her hiking boots planted on the bench.

"Sing me a song to soothe my weary soul," I said to her,

laying my head down.

She started playing a hypnotic picking pattern and then started singing - really belting it out. She sang like an Appalachian Indie-Pop diva. The song she sang to me dealt with giving her heart to someone, and then having that person eat it like Valentine's candy. By the time she finished, I was sitting upright on my elbows, watching in an almost trance-like state. She had me wrapped around her little picking finger.

"That was great," I said. "Did you write that?"

"Yes," she answered. "I call that 'I Gave You My Heart and You Ate It.'"

"Play another."

She broke into a banjo blues song and crooned:

You wrote your name in the wet cement of my heart,
And it dried just in time for us to part.

After she finished I said, "That was really good too, but also kind of depressing. Do you write any happy songs?"

"I wrote one once. But that song depresses me more than all the others. I write mostly breakup songs because I'm good at it."

"You're good at breaking up with people?"

"No. Well, maybe, but I know I'm good at writing breakup songs."

With that I lay back down and drifted off to sleep while Trouble was gently plucking away.

When I woke up, I was alone at the campsite. It must have been five or six in the evening. The van was still there, that was a good sign. I lit a small fire and cooked up some coffee in my French press and a can of baked beans from my food cache. After finishing about half of the coffee and beans, I grabbed Meal-ticket and started rehearsing some originals I was working on. Sitting, watching the fire die, I began mindlessly strumming a slow song called 'Pirouettes.' The song was a five-minute philosophic ramble. I let the last chord ring out and was on the verge of beginning another song when she startled me.

"That was beautiful. Did you write that?" Lauren asked from behind me.

I almost fell off the picnic table bench. "Jesus, Lauren. You scared the shit out of me. How long were you standing there?"

"Long enough. I just got back from a little hike." She sat down next to me, and started helping herself to the rest of the beans and coffee. "Did you write that?"

"Yup."

"Well play another."

So I played a couple more; a love song and a hobo song. She listened to them intently, contently eating my beans and drinking my coffee beans. She was done eating after my second song, and I started putting the guitar away.

"You write some pretty good songs," she said to me.

"Well thanks. You're not so bad yourself."

"How come you don't play your originals at the bars to raise gas money?"

"Sometimes I do. It's got to be the right kind of crowd for that though."

"Well I think any old crowd would appreciate a song that you actually felt and wrote more than hearing the same old 'Blueberry Hill' or 'Time of Your Life' again."

I smirked. "You might think so, but no."

"Why don't they just put the radio on instead then? What's the real difference?"

"Sometimes I wonder that myself. But I'm always happy to step up and be a jukebox. Otherwise I'd truly be broke, and we wouldn't be able to get to Wisconsin."

With that I slid Meal-ticket into the van. "Speaking of which," I said "these instruments aren't going to raise money on their own. I think the nearest town, West Yellowstone, might have a place we can play if you're up for it."

"Okay," she said and downed the rest of the coffee like a shot of whiskey.

The whole ride out of Yellowstone and into town I had visions of Bonnie and Clyde in my head – a friendly version for the modern world. We wouldn't rob banks, we'd rob people's hearts. They wouldn't be able to help tipping us all the cash they were carrying - writing checks too. We might even have to invest in a credit card machine.

We ambled into a place called The Wagon Inn. On that night, it was home to a gambling tournament. I introduced Lauren as my wife, and we got the go-ahead to play.

It wasn't a very busy bar. The majority of the people there were gambling at a long green table near the back. So I chose a booth near the gambling table, and started unpacking. Lauren set her banjo on the ground and plopped into a seat at the booth next to mine.

I was confused. "What's up? We going to jam or what?"

"I don't jam."

"What?"

"I'm a self-taught banjo player. I have no idea what I'm doing. I can't jam."

"But I heard you earlier. You're really good. Come on over and strut your stuff."

"Nope. I only play banjo on my originals."

"Well how about singing with me then? You said we killed the other night."

"I don't know all the words to those songs you cover. I mean, I've heard most of them, but I don't know them well enough to perform."

"But you said we sang Dylan and Sublime the other night."

"Those are two I do know."

"Well come on up, we'll start with those two."

Lauren grudgingly got up and stood next to me. We got through a shaky version of 'Don't Think Twice, It's All Right' and chased it with a slightly stronger version of 'What I Got' for an audience that did not seem to want to acknowledge our existence, or else were too into their hands of poker to notice.

"See? You're a natural," I said to Lauren. She reacted with a grimace that suggested she was not having fun.

After playing a round of twenty questions with her, we

figured out that we both knew the majority of the words to 'Stand By Me' which got some applause from the folks at the bar. I was starting to figure out how to harmonize with her.

"I'm going to take a break now," Lauren said, and she walked away from me. I watched her take a seat, open up her banjo case, and pull a ridiculous looking self-help book out of it. She started reading.

"Let's hear it for my wife, Lauren," I said to the audience. She got a smattering of claps, set her book down for a moment, and flashed a fake smile at the people playing cards. She quickly turned back to me with an evil eye before going back to reading.

I launched into a typical cover set, starting with a version of Kenny Rogers' 'The Gambler.' This got them going a little bit more, and a few people stepped up to tip. I was hoping that like the winner on the slots in South Dakota, whoever won big here tonight would not forget to tip his lucky charm minstrels.

Lauren was on her second or third free beer when I decided to take a break. "Play your banjo for the kind folks," I said as I walked past her to the bar.

She stepped up and played a beautiful, tragic love song based around a metaphor involving board games. Then she played a short number about a divorce that included a lot of cussing. The swearing got a rise out of some fellows and they threw a dollar or two down. Then Lauren took a seat and the bar was silent except for the sound of poker chips changing hands. I made a B-Line back to my guitar and started singing a Van Morrison song, and Lauren wandered out of the bar and into the night with her banjo.

I finished about an hour later with close to forty dollars and walked back to the van. Lauren was curled up in the passenger seat.

"Get your gas money?" she asked in a tone.

"Yeah. Thanks for all the help."

Out of nowhere I saw Lauren's fist come flying at me. She nailed me in the arm.

"Really?! Really. What the hell is your deal?" I shouted,

rubbing my shoulder.

"You ass! I can't do what you do."

"You can do it just fine. You just gotta loosen up a bit is all."

"But did you see the way they ignored me tonight? I can't stand being ignored when I play."

"Listen, Lauren. You're cute and all, but you can't expect to be the center of attention all the time. We are musicians. We are going to be just background ambiance sometimes. A lot of times. It's part of the game."

"But people don't tip for me. They want to hear cover songs, and I don't know any. And anyway, I don't want to go in front of people and be some sort of dancing bear. I write my own songs. I'm an artist."

That one cut a little bit.

"So I'm a big dancing bear? I write my own songs too. And they aren't all crying in my beer breakup songs. But you - you're an artist." Lauren turned away from me. "You know what, even if I am a dancing bear, who says that a dancing bear isn't an artist?" She was silent, and I was too wound up to stop now. "This is supposed to be fun..."

She interrupted, "It doesn't seem like fun when our survival and mode of transportation depend on it."

"True, Lauren. It has some serious aspects. Like a job. But unlike most jobs, I'm having fun doing this."

"I'm not."

"Are you trying to not have fun? People are paying us to play music. We could be stuck in some stuffy office somewhere, but we're in West Yellowstone playing music. Stop pissing on my dancing bear parade!"

"Take me back to the campsite."

"So much for the great adventures of the new Bonnie and Clyde," I said to myself while fumbling with my keys.

"TAKE ME BACK!"

We drove in silence. I've had some silences with people before. I would call this an awkward one. I was worried she might have been crying. I could hear her sniffling occasionally, but couldn't bring myself to look at her. I cut the engine when we got to the campsite and we both just sat there.

"I don't even know who Bonnie and Clyde are," she said quietly.

"What!? What were you under a rock for the entirety of the 1930s? Did you avoid movie theaters in the 60s?" I snapped, half-jokingly.

She was humorless. "Where are you sleeping tonight?" she asked.

"The tent."

"Good. Get out. I'm sleeping here."

"Good. I wouldn't have it any other way."

"Good."

I pocketed the van keys, slammed the door, and crawled into the tent.

I woke up when the sun reached the tent and started cooking me. Rolling out of the oven, I was surprised to see Lauren already awake. She was making coffee and cooking oatmeal over a small fire. The smell of the morning dew in the sun mingled with the fire and coffee, and for a brief moment I felt good.

"You only have one cup," she said. "So you can have the first one. Oatmeal will be ready soon."

She must have really made herself at home in the van, having found the dishes and food boxes. I remember thinking that maybe the new day wouldn't just be a horrible continuation of the night before, and I wouldn't have to leave her at an airport somewhere.

"Thanks."

She handed me a fork, put the hot pan of oatmeal down on the picnic table, and sat next to me. Then she dug into the oatmeal with a spoon and motioned for me to do the same with my fork. This was nice. I didn't fully trust it, but we finished off the pan and passed the solitary cup of coffee back and forth. Except for the birds flitting through the trees around camp, this was all done in silence. Those birds were too cheery for the morning - they always are.

"Thanks for cooking breakfast."

"You're welcome."

It was going to be a hot day. I was wondering what we were

going to do with it.

"Ben," said Lauren, turning to me.

"Lauren," I said meeting her eyes straight on.

"I'm sorry for punching you in the arm last night."

I suppressed a chuckle and said, "Yeah, well I'm sorry I was mean to you. I said some things in a fit of anger, and they shouldn't have been said. I don't really know what I was thinking overall anyway. I work alone."

She looked out at those cheery asshole birds and then back to me.

"Yeah. Well, I write some music and pick my banjo, and I do consider it to be an art, but I'm not a musician. I'm a Geology major."

I drained the last of the coffee as she continued. "Music is my hobby. It's just... I wanted so badly to impress you. I was hoping I might earn my keep on this trip with music. I thought I'd be able to do things that I couldn't do when the time came."

We watched those little birds chasing each other through the trees. They had no idea what was happening in the world around them. It was like they didn't even care.

Lauren turned back to me. "It certainly didn't help that you were such an asshole."

I rolled my eyes. "Listen, we were both in the wrong last night. I was an asshole and you were a bitch. We're both sorry now. Let's just call it even. Forgive and forget." I stood up with the pan and coffee fixings and started walking towards the water spigot to wash them off. "And anyway," I said to her over my back, "I'm already impressed with you. So stop trying to impress me. Just relax." I started rinsing the pan. "Hey! Let's explore this park today."

"Really!?"

"Well we're here aren't we?"

"Thank you! Thank you! You have no idea how much I want to see Old Faithful shoot off his load."

I turned and squinted my eyes at her questioningly. She gave me a big smile and just shrugged her shoulders. 'Today might be worth staying awake for,' I thought to myself.

We saw the faithful one ejaculate right on schedule. We saw the sulfurous tie dye rainbows of the Morning Glory Pool. We saw the Martian-like terrain of Mammoth Springs. We saw a marmot, and it barked at us. We toured around the park like a couple of old married folks, Lauren snapping pictures at every stop. We even drove the van through a herd of buffalo. They were using the road as a trail.

"We're so close to these buffalo, we could reach out the window and touch them," I said.

"We're so close to these buffalo, we could hop out of this van and ride them like a boxcar," Lauren said.

"We're so close to these buffalo, we could feed them breath mints. Because we can smell their breath... and it's bad," I lamely retorted.

"We're so close to these buffalo, we're inside them," she said.

I laughed. "All right. You win."

We saw all the geological features we could fit into one day before we got back to the campsite where I made a feast of tuna macaroni and cheese. Lauren found my emergency bourbon flask under the driver's seat and cracked it open for us.

I was sitting on the ground strumming Meal-ticket in the fire light after dinner. "You know what Lauren, you're not half bad when you aren't trying to impress anyone." I was starting to feel the emergency bourbon merge into my system.

"You're not so bad yourself, when you keep your mouth shut, Ben."

We both laughed and then she said, "Hey, play me one of those original songs of yours that never raise any gas money."

I grinned in the dark. "All right. I'll play you my drinking song. I wrote this here thing about my first, my third... " I paused and looked thoughtfully up at the column of smoke rising from the fire up to the stars, "and my second wife, in that order. Hell, if you're lucky, someday it might be about you too."

I played my song for Lauren. It had an old-timey country feel to it, like a Hank Williams song, and a terribly catchy drink-and-sing-along chorus. By the end, Lauren had picked up the words to the chorus and sang along with me:

You don't like talking to me when I'm drinking.
I don't like talking to you when I'm sober.
So let's agree to disagree and call the thing over.

After we finished, people in the next campsite applauded.

"Thank you!" I said loudly in their direction. "I'm selling CDs too. Come on over if you like."

Sure enough, two fellows from Texas made their way through the brush to us. We chatted with them for a bit. I played a short campfire set. Even Lauren grabbed her banjo and picked a number. I ended up selling three CDs to them, and they gave me some contact info to use if I ever found myself in the Dallas region.

The fire died down, and I went to the camp bathroom to ready myself for bed. When I got back, I was surprised to find Lauren already in the tent.

"Am I in the van tonight?" I asked her.

"No. It gets cold sleeping alone. Come in here."

I crawled in and wrapped my arms around her. "Hello, stranger," I said.

She turned away from me and whispered sleepily, "Don't get any ideas, Buster. Let's just spoon."

The little dipper smiled down at our kitchen drawer tent as we spooned to stay warm in the Yellowstone night.

I watched the dollar signs roll by as I filled up the van's gas tank outside of Sturgis, South Dakota. It was like playing a slot machine that I simply could not win. Lauren was asleep in the passenger seat. She hadn't really chipped in any money yet. She wasn't trying to be sneaky about it. She knew I knew, but I don't think she really had any money to spare. And since I was enjoying her company, and headed to Wisconsin anyway, I decided to let it slide.

After a small fight over the radio, we landed on a solid 'road rule': the driver chooses tunes. So I picked a huge mix of Townes Van Zandt and Neil Young to listen to. I was going to drive until the mix ran out or until we got to the Badlands, whichever came first. We got to the Badlands first.

Lauren woke up when I was paying the entrance fee and chatting with the ranger lady running the booth.

"Are there any good places to camp here tonight?" I asked the ranger.

"Well, there's the free campground a little ways in, but it's about a ten-mile drive down a dirt road."

"Van can take it," I said patting the dash board. "Where is it at?"

The ranger showed me on the map as Lauren rubbed her eyes, and those green globes came back to life. I thanked the ranger and we drove into the park towards free camping.

"Where are we?" Lauren yawned.

"We're in the Badlands."

"Where's that?"

"Come on, Geology major. The Badlands National Park of South Dakota."

The Badlands mark the end of the Rocky Mountain Foothills and the start of the Midwest plains. It's like the plains just sort of crack open out of massive, twisting canyons and dirt mountains.

After following the map a ways down a gravely road (it was like driving on the voice of Tom Waits), we found the free campground. It was a small circular prairie surrounded by large hills on prime buffalo-feeding territory. During the day, the giant beasts would sort of hang out along the perimeter of the campground. At night the buffalo would move in to feed.

There weren't really campsites per se. It was just the open plains, and you could stake a claim on any spot that was available. We stuck a flag into the land and pretended to be prairie land homesteaders. The wind had whipped itself into a fury that evening, and although it would have rather been a parachute or a sail, Lauren and I wrestled the tent until it was standing properly.

We explored the campground and found trails that led up around the hills. "You want to go on a hike with me?" I asked Lauren.

"Sure," she said with a smile, and she grabbed a water bottle. We took the trail nearest to our tent and hiked uphill, pausing every so often to wait for a buffalo that seemed too close to move on. The park had really horrific signs posted along the roads with illustrations of how a buffalo can gore a human.

"So Ben, how long are you going to stay in Wisconsin? What are your big plans?" Lauren asked me.

"Planning is such a pain for me, Lauren. I try to take it one day at a time."

"I see. So you have nothing planned for Wisconsin?"

"Well, I want to rest. I'm burnt out on this road thing at the moment. I just want to find a safe place to lay low for a few weeks and recover. I'll figure it out from there. What about you?"

"Ohhh, I'll move back into my efficiency apartment. School starts back up in three or four weeks. Hopefully I'll be able to get my job at the coffee shop back."

I was starting to get a little winded. She seemed to be getting there too. I slowed down, but she kept going at her faster pace. She was sitting at the top of the hill, sipping from her water bottle when I caught up to her.

"You know, for an alcoholic you're in pretty good shape," I coughed as I sat down next to her.

She smiled at me as her hair blew in the wind, flowing around her face as if it had a life of its own. "What do you want to be when you grow up?" she asked.

"I am grown up. This is it."

"Really? This is what you want to be doing? I mean you're going back to Wisconsin because you seem tired of it."

"Yeah. I get tired of it sometimes and need a break. Maybe I'm just scraping by at the moment, but I'm making a living being a musician. I have the rest of my life to worry about finding a permanent place to live, maybe having a family, and getting some kind of steady job, but now is my time to adventure forth and see the world. I got a van and a guitar. I got my health, so why not?"

"I suppose you'll figure out what to do after this when you get too tired of being a road musician to go back to it."

"If I ever get completely fed up with this musician thing, then yes. But for now the plan is not to plan until I need a plan. Planning takes all the fun out of the future. What about you? What can you do with geology? You going to be a miner?"

"Actually there's some tech work for geologists in the oil industry."

"Really? Maybe you could chip in for gas by drilling the next tank out of these Badlands," I snickered.

"Hey! I'll be able to throw you a couple bucks when we get back to La Crosse."

"It's all right. I'm only kidding," I said laughing and bumping my shoulder against hers.

We sat up there in the wind, watching the buffalo shadows

grow longer. Suddenly, right as the sun was setting, Lauren jumped on top of me, and her lips pressed against mine.

It was after dark by the time we headed back to camp, but an almost-full moon lit the way. The tent broke while we were hiking. The support poles snapped under the weight of the wind, and it had collapsed on itself. So that was how the tent ended.

We tried to fix it best we could with duct tape in the moonlight. One pole worked properly but the other could only prop halfway up. The effect was something between a glorified sleeping bag and a deflated beach ball. We made ourselves at home and picked up where we had left off at the top of the hill.

I had removed Lauren's shirt and was working on her bra, when a large shadow in the moonlight crossed the wall of our broken down tent.

"What is it?" Lauren asked, puzzled and slightly panicked.

"I think our privacy is being invaded."

"By who?"

"A buffalo."

We listened as the shadow munched away on the lush campground grass near us.

"I'm okay with it if you are," Lauren said beneath me.

I was okay with it too, and we quietly continued on our journey to the promised land in the shadow of the mighty buffalo.

I was at the wheel of the van and we were about thirty miles outside the Wisconsin border when Lauren turned to me and asked, "What's going to happen to us when we get there?"

"Us?"

"Yeah. You and me."

"I thought I would drop you off at your apartment. You'd go your way, and I'd go mine."

"You know you're welcome to stay and relax a few days at my place if you want."

"Thanks. I'll consider that."

"Do you think if you ever found the right girl, you might settle down and stay in one place?"

I didn't like where the conversation was headed. "Maybe someday. But if I found the right girl right now, I don't think we'd settle down. I think she'd saddle up and hit the road with me."

"You sure ask a lot of the right girl. You might end up an old maid because of it."

I scoffed at this comment and started fiddling with the radio to put some Dylan on.

Lauren continued, "What if the right girl couldn't hit the road at the moment, but you needed a break anyway, and she offered you a nice place to crash."

I snapped a little. "Lauren, you're a great gal. We've had a lot of fun together, but I just don't think you are the right girl."

She was quiet after that. She didn't move for a couple of minutes as I tried to get the radio to work. Then she dug through the debris around her seat, picked up her journal, and started writing.

Except for Dylan singing his bitter 'It's All Over Now, Baby Blue' love songs and the sound of the wheels peeling along the highway, we rode in silence into La Crosse, Wisconsin. Lauren directed me to her apartment. It was an efficiency on the second floor of a cute little Victorian house about a mile from the historic downtown and two miles from the Mississippi River. I pulled up next to her yard and parked in the road, keeping the motor running.

"You need help carrying your things up there?" I asked.

"No," she said, trying to gather all her scattered belongings from the van. Once she accomplished that amazing feat, she opened her door as if to leave, but turned back to face me instead. "I just wrote a song. Doesn't have music yet. Do you want to hear the words?"

"Okay." This was a trap and I knew it.

She dug the journal back out of her bag, opened it to the most recent pages and started reading. Not only did she condemn my drinking, she admonished me for having misled her and for being some sort of lying asshole. She even lifted some lines from my 'Pirouettes' song. She finished up her piece and looked at me straight-faced.

For a moment I was actually speechless, but I quickly found my tongue. "Where to start, Lauren? Should I start with the fact that you bring up my drinking like it's a problem when you drink just as much as I do? In fact, I've been drinking more since I met you. Should I start with the fact that I always told the truth and never once led you on? I may be an asshole, but it's not for lying. Or should I start with the blatant plagiarism of one of my songs?"

I was trying to be calm but this was all a little much for me. "As a matter of fact, I've been nothing but good to you since I met you. I gave you a free ride across the country, I fed and took care of you, and this is how you repay me? By vilifying me in a song that you already plagiarized me with? I'm sorry if you feel as bad as those lyrics describe, but honey, grow up."

With that she shoved her journal back into her bag, grabbed her banjo from the back of the van and slammed the doors shut.

As she crossed her yard I shouted, "You wrote us a breakup song, and we weren't even going out!" and punched the gas out of La Crosse.

I held the pedal to the floor until I got midway through the state, to a college town called Steven's Point. 'Now I can actually start relaxing and get back to being road ready,' I thought to myself, 'maybe even record some music.'

An old high school buddy of mine named Mike was currently living in Steven's Point. I met up with him at his house, and we decided to go knock a couple back at the bars on the main drag. It started off innocent enough, but ended in a week-long, blackout drunk, statewide binge. Every place I went turned into a welcome back and a farewell party, as I would only stay for a night or two in any one place.

I remember on that first night there were cops heavily patrolling the bar scene. Drunk people, young and old were shuffling freely through the street, like it was a giant hallway with walls made of old brick buildings.

We weren't planning on driving, but as we walked under the street lights past where Mike had parked his pickup, I noticed a "No Parking between 2 AM and 6 AM" sign.

"Mike, you're going to get a ticket tonight."

"What?"

"That sign by your truck." I pointed it out.

"Are you serious? Two o'clock is bar close. It's like they're encouraging drunken driving."

I knew I couldn't drive because Mike had kept me swimming in beer all night, but I wasn't sure about him. Mike wasn't sure either. We saw a cop car parked across the road, and he decided to get a legal answer. I stood by his truck as he waltzed over.

"Hello sir," Mike said to the cop through his open window. "Sorry to bother you, but I was wondering if I could get a breathalyzer to see if I can drive my truck home or if I should walk."

The cop did a double take, then nodded, grabbed the breathalyzer and stepped out of his vehicle. Sure enough, Mike was too drunk to drive.

"You see," Mike said to the cop, "my truck is parked where it's not supposed to be between two and six. I didn't know the spot was designated like that. Do you think if I left it, I would get a parking ticket?"

"Probably."

"How much are parking tickets here?"

"Thirty-five dollars."

"I can't afford that," Mike said. "Would it be all right if we didn't start the truck, but pushed it to a parking spot that it won't get ticketed in?"

"No," the cop said deadpan.

Mike walked back over to where I was leaning on his truck. "What's the verdict?" I asked.

He didn't seem to listen, just walked past and peeked around the first side street about half a block down. Then he walked back to me.

"Verdict is, we wait for the cops to leave and then push this truck over to that first turn, where we're free to park anywhere."

So we waited about twenty minutes, making fun of ourselves and the stumbling drunks on their way to oblivion, keeping a watchful eye on the truck and the cops. Eventually the cop Mike spoke to slowly drove off.

"It's on!" Mike announced, dashing to the driver's side, popping the truck into neutral and pocketing the keys. "As long as the keys aren't in the ignition, I don't think we're doing anything wrong."

With both doors open, we pushed his pickup backwards through the shouting crowd. We took a wide left onto the side street. Mike was steering us back to the curb when the same cop pulled around the corner and almost rammed into the truck.

"What the hell are you doing?" the cop yelled at us through his window.

"I can't afford a parking ticket," Mike said.

"But I told you NOT to do that," the cop said.

"Well should we just leave it here in the middle of the road now or what?"

The policeman shook his head slowly without taking his eyes off of Mike. "Go park it," he said.

We pushed the truck into a good spot. Mike put it back into park, and locked the doors.

Another cop car pulled up and stopped right next to our policeman. They started talking, and Mike walked over to try and explain himself to the new cop, but before he could get a word out, the first one shouted, "If you know what's good for you, you'll keep moving." Mike turned right around, and we walked back to his house to crash. But I kept moving.

I met up with my friend Bob at his parents' cabin somewhere in the middle of nowhere, Wisconsin. He was shooting an independent slasher movie in the wilderness, and I was supposed to hold the microphone and deal with sound. When I got there, I found that my job had already been filled, so I bought a bottle of whiskey, and transformed my job from sound guy to whiskey boy. It was actually like being a water boy in a drunken football game. Whenever tensions rose, I dashed onto the scene with my handle of whiskey to diffuse the situation with a healthy dose of good team spirits.

It was at the end of one of those nights, when everyone was already passed out except for me, an actress, and an actor, that I got some sort of drunken poetic notion in my head. I don't remember it, but the other two said that it was actually kind of deep. It should be noted that they were both very drunk.

The actor described it thusly: "Everything was fine, and kind of calm. You were lying on the ground - I thought you were falling asleep," he told me. "You were lying by the can of silver spray paint we used for the plastic machetes, and then you suddenly yelled the title of some Tom Wolfe novel, reached out and grabbed the can of spray paint, and then dashed to the road shouting about 'wise words, needing to be spoken.'"

There was a Wisconsin State Highway in front of the cabin. It was a fairly unpopulated area of Wisconsin, so the driveway was the only one for about a half mile in either direction.

The actor continued, "I was chasing behind you, but you had a head start on me. By the time I caught up, you had spray-painted half of a giant ten-foot heart across a lane of the highway. I remember telling you that Bob and his folks probably wouldn't like finding graffiti right in front of their cabin. This gave you pause. You stood up, took a step back, and looked at your work. Then you told me that you just couldn't do a job halfheartedly, and filled the other lane with the other half."

I don't remember passing out, but I do remember Bob tapping on the van window to wake me up the next day. He seemed chipper. I slouched out of the van and said, "Hey... I'm sorry, but I think I may have spray painted the highway last night."

"What?"

"I don't know if it actually happened. My recollection is a little shaky. But there might be a two-lane silver heart spray painted on the highway in front of this driveway."

He looked at me and just shook his head. Then he walked out to the road. I started rummaging through the van for water. When he got back, he slapped me in the face.

He was furious. "My dad will kill me. You need to fix this today."

So I drove to the nearest hardware store and got two gallons of turpentine and a metal wire brush. That buggy night found me out on the highway with the brush, turpentine, whiskey, and a flashlight. While the others celebrated finishing the movie, I bent over and scrubbed off the spray paint. I had to dash to the shoulder of the road when cars drove past. I wonder how that must have looked to the late night Wisconsin drivers.

"Did you see that guy? Did he have a gallon of turpentine in one hand and a gallon of whiskey in the other?"

After several hours of scrubbing and cursing, the road was as clean as it was going to get. Bob's folks never mentioned it to him, so I figure it must have been good enough. That sort of shit always happens to me though: I give my heart out to the world and then end up scraping it off the pavement. It could have been in one of Lauren's songs.

A day or two later I was in the town of Sturgeon Bay on Lake Michigan. My friend Rick and I were drunk, scoping out rummage sales. I found a fancy antique set of six mini liquor bottle sake shots. The bottles in the set were all decorated to look like little geishas, and they all still had the original flavored forty-year-old sake in it. If you ask me, it was a steal at two dollars. At the next stop I found an old combination-lock briefcase. Because the owners didn't know the combo, I got it for free. Who knows what could have been in there: stolen art? Beef jerky?

We brought it back to Rick and his wife Sarah's house where I took a butcher knife and butchered my way into the brief case. Through the big hole I found nothing but an old business card, so I shoved in the antique sake bottles and we left to attend to business in the Sturgeon Bay bar district. On the sidewalk at some point, I cracked open one of those little bottles. Over time it had turned into a disgusting, sugary syrup. I still finished it though. Two dollars is two dollars. I ended up handing the majority of the rest of those bottles out to strangers I met in the street.

I had 300 dollars set aside in my savings account. This was for emergencies. Because Rick and Sarah were letting me crash at their house, I decided buying them drinks for the night was emergency enough, and took 200 dollars out of an ATM. I started storing the cash in the busted brief case, so every time I purchased a drink, I had to set the brief case on the bar and pull money out of its hole. I thought it made me look very important - like a businessman on a very important bender.

The last thing I vaguely remember was sitting on a draw bridge over Lake Michigan, screaming 'The Wreck of the Edmund Fitzgerald' at the top of my lungs. I closed my eyes and chucked something as far as I could. When I opened them, I saw my briefcase sinking into the murky depths of Lake Michigan. Some scattered bills floated out of the hole to the surface.

I woke up and knew it was all wrong. I came back to Wisconsin to recuperate and I was in worse shape than ever. I didn't say goodbye. I just got into the van and started driving. The road in front of the van led me back across the state, through Steven's Point and up into La Crosse. The ride ended in front of Lauren's house at about six in the morning.

"You look like shit," Lauren said when she answered the door.

"My guns are down. Can I crash here for a couple days?"

"Come in. Come in," she said.

*

I slept restlessly in her bed. I don't know how long I was lying there. Lauren came and went, the sun did the same. One morning I woke up and Lauren was bringing a steaming bowl of chicken noodle soup over to me. She sat on the edge of the bed as I cooled spoonfuls of soup by blowing on them.

"You've been asleep for days. I was worried you were dead."

"I do that sometimes," I said slurping down a spoon.

"What happened?" she asked.

"The opposite of what I intended. I outdrank the world."

She got up and started changing out of her pajamas and into some street clothes. "I'm going to head off to work at my coffee shop," she said. "You get some rest, and I'll be back in a few hours." She was halfway out the door when she turned back to me, her dark pony tail flying behind her head. "And I know we sort of left on a sour note ... when I wrote and recited that song to you ..."

I chuckled and dribbled soup down my chin. "Yeah, it took some balls for you to read that to me, but I understand. And really, I'm just happy I could inspire someone."

"We left on a bad note," she went on, "but I want you to know that you are welcome to stay here as long as you like. Make yourself at home." Then she quickly shut the door and was gone.

After I downed the soup, I explored her little efficiency apartment. It was two small rooms really, if you didn't include the closet with the bathroom in it. The one room by the front door was a pastel-yellow kitchen. It felt like 1950 in there - like Beaver Cleaver might come busting in the door any moment. The other room was a bedroom/family room hybrid, had fake wood paneling, and a futon that served as a bed. There was an old record player sitting next to an older TV on a little bookshelf across from the bed. Lauren's book collection was on the shelves below. I inspected them and was happy to see that there was some Tom Robbins and Mark Twain inhabiting those shelves. The lowest shelf was filled to the brim with self-help books.

I haphazardly grabbed one of the self-help books, got comfortable on the floor, and started to read it. Moments later I passed out again. When I woke up, I picked up the book and resumed where I had left off. The passage that followed sort of jumped out at me. It read: "Sometimes it is necessary to do something completely different; an action that seems completely opposite from what you usually do, simply because it is something you don't usually do."

I closed the book and put it back in its spot. Then I grabbed Meal-ticket and stared long and hard at the front door in the kitchen. I saw the door handle turn, and Lauren walked in.

"Whatcha doing, Ben? How you feeling?"

I set Meal-ticket down. "I feel a little better."

"You going somewhere?"

"Why?"

"I rented some movies. I thought we might order a pizza and chug a beer or two." She set her keys and a couple movies down on the stove. "You in?"

"Yeah. Sure. I'm in tonight."

That night turned into a couple nights. It was pleasant in a domestic sort of way, but it wasn't long until the itch came back. I couldn't avoid it. I heard it every time a train went past. I heard it every time I looked at my van, sitting like a beached whale at the curb. The road was calling me.

Early one morning, with her asleep in bed next to me, I slid out of the covers, walked past her self-help books, grabbed

Meal-ticket and tiptoed towards the door.

"Ben?" Lauren called after me. "What are you doing?"

"Lauren," I started hesitantly. "Thanks for letting me stay here a while to recuperate, but I think it's time I hit that old trail. Besides I don't want to become a drag on you or stuff up this little place."

"You aren't a drag. I want you to stay. Come back to bed."

"I'm sorry Lauren," I said opening the door.

A silence filled the space between us that seemed to drag through a couple of lifetimes. "You're a coward," Lauren hissed at me.

"Excuse me?"

"You're always leaving - always running away. You've already roamed this country, Ben. Now take a risk and stay here with me."

All my instincts were screaming 'NO! Get the hell out of Dodge!' But when I opened my mouth, the only word that plopped out was "Okay."

I closed the door, climbed back into bed, and squeezed Lauren tight against me.

A couple weeks passed as Lauren and I got used to each other. The weeks piled up into months, and it started to feel like we had always lived in that little apartment together, snug as bugs in a rug of love, taking slugs from a big wine jug. I started booking shows all around town at any place that wanted music. I even played at a thrift shop in exchange for some T-shirts.

One of the better shows I played was at the La Crosse Hyatt. I was singing a handful of slightly raunchier, double entendre-filled country and blues songs - like Johnny Cash with the sensibilities of a sailor. The guests at the bar of their diamond-chandelier hotel didn't pay me much mind. They were busy drinking ten-dollar Martinis and commenting on each others' suits and dresses. I still had a brief moral dilemma at the end of the night, as I internally debated whether or not I should play a particularly coarse song written by the Moldy Peaches called 'Who's Got the Crack?' Not wanting to be weighed down by any regrets, I made it the closing song of the night. I thought it would be nice to go out with an inappropriate bang. After the last chord had stopped resonating to an interesting mixture of applause and disgust, a serious-looking blonde manager lady came up to me, arms folded, anger spreading across her face like the oncoming clouds of a thunderstorm.

"We've had some complaints about your subject matter," she huffed. "I'm going to have to ask you to either change your subject matter or leave."

I glanced over at the clock on the lounge wall. "Well technically the time I was under contract for has passed. So I think I'll just leave. Where can I pick up my check?"

I left bubbling over with laughter, one hand holding Lauren's hand and the other holding a big, fat corporate check. The La Crosse Hyatt never booked me again, but I was OK with that.

I played a lot of shows at Lauren's coffee shop. I was trying to work the tip money angle a little more, so I wrote a song called 'Out of Necessity' specifically designed to bring in some dough. It went something like:

> *If everyone chips in just a dollar or ten,*
> *I would go to the store and start eating again.*
> *I'd get out of bed, and pay my rent,*
> *I wouldn't blow it all on alcohol and cigarettes.*
> *I take requests, yes I will, write it on the back of a*
> *   hundred-dollar bill.*
> *Open up your heart and empty your pockets.*

This song became my closer at every one of those cafe shows. Someone actually dropped a $100 bill into my coffee can tip jar one night. Despite making money out of music, I was still barely covering my expenses.

One night while lying in bed, Lauren turned to me. "Ben?"

"Yes, Lauren."

"I go to school, work a job, and occasionally play gigs with you."

"Yes, and I find it all very impressive."

"I'm starting to get sick of you sitting around the apartment and doing whatever it is you do all the time."

"I'm busy with a lot of different music projects, you know that."

"Yeah. But I'm sick of the fact that we can't afford anything to eat except Ramen noodles. I asked you to stay Ben, and

I'm glad you did. But now I'm asking you to please consider getting a job."

"I can't get a job," I told her. "I'm too busy right now. Being unemployed is a full-time job."

She rolled her eyes and then her body followed suit as she rolled away from me.

The first job I found was through a temp agency. I was a glorified janitor on a construction site. They gave me a broom, a hard hat, and nine dollars an hour to sweep up after the messes that come with building a five-story condo downtown.

Wherever my broom and I would go, a cloud of dust and dirt would follow. I was like a character from the Peanuts cartoon. The other workers didn't like having me around them because I made the construction site look like the dustbowl whenever I swept past.

The basement was both a parking garage and a home for local bats. I'd find a dead one every so often as I swept. Like a hackneyed bat undertaker, or angel of bat death, I would sweep their grimy, twisted bodies off the ground and throw them into a garbage can coffin. None of them ever had a look of peace on their face.

As the job came nearer to completion, there were fewer messes to sweep up. Even though my job for all practical purposes had ended, the supervisors kept me on, either to help me out financially, or else out of sheer laziness. I would do whatever odd jobs they had so they could spend their time talking dirty to the cleaning ladies who had been enlisted to start a major vacuuming and dusting campaign on the place. I cored the concrete roof beams for a while, and then I was put to work replacing every step in the building, because the first time they were installed it wasn't done to code.

Then one day there was nothing else to be done, so they sent me home. I kept the garage door opener to the bat cave with the intention of breaking in late one night for a big jam session with Lauren and some other friends, but it never quite panned out.

There was a pawn shop about five blocks from the apartment. One evening, after hearing a parade of emergency sirens go by, I turned on the news and saw that the pawn shop had been held up, and a high-speed chase was ensuing. A few days later, I was out for a walk and noticed that the pawn shop now had a "Help Wanted" sign in its front window. I had just finished the construction gig, so I figured what the hell? I waltzed in and picked up an application.

I remember telling Lauren later that night, "I'm going to get a job there. I'm overqualified and they will hire me." It took the pawn shop three weeks to get back to me, but they finally called and set up an interview. I was confident as shit when I met the owners, and sure as shit, I landed the job.

On my first day a disheveled guy walked in with a couple pool sticks. He set the sticks on the counter and said, "I gotta get my brother out of jail." He shook his head as my boss inspected the pool cues.

"Ridiculous," the disheveled fellow went on. "My dad calls me and tells me to bail him out. Had it been me, they would have left me in jail and said I should have known better. But it's my little brother."

My boss was on the computer looking up the pool cues on eBay. This particular pawn shop no longer used 'Blue Book Pricing.' We used eBay on a blue computer. When my boss found similar or matching items, he offered a third of what the item sold for, and then turned around and sold it for the eBay price.

"I can give you seventy bucks for these pool sticks," he said.

"You can't do better than that? These are top of the line, man."

"Seventy bucks. Take it or leave it."

"All right. That will do. Maybe I'll take a peek around the store anyway though."

A few minutes later the fellow came back to the front counter with his seventy dollars in one hand and a thirty-dollar CB radio in the other.

"I'm going to tell them I could only get forty for his bail," he said grinning and laying thirty dollars down.

Valentine's Day at the shop was an interesting day too. A flood of guys came rushing in throughout the day to browse our fine jewelry selection. One fellow sort of pulled a reversal though. He walked right up to the register and pulled his wedding band off.

"How much can I get for this?" he asked us.

My boss looked the ring over. "I can give you ten dollars for this. But the state will tax you two bucks."

"So you'll give me eight dollars then?"

"Yes."

"I'll take it. At least I will have gotten something out of the marriage."

Lauren came into the apartment one afternoon while I was staring blankly at my van out the window.

"Today was my last day of classes for a while. What should we do?"

The van was just sitting there. It looked unhappy. "Let's go to Alaska," I said as a serious joke.

"Okay," Lauren replied.

When I turned from the window I found her at the laptop typing furiously. "What are you doing?" I asked her.

"I'm finding us work in Alaska."

After a good five-minute search on the World Wide Web, we were both e-mailing our resumes to a salmon processing plant. Brook Leader Fisheries called three hours later and conducted phone interviews on the spot. The ball was in motion, and moving rather quickly. We were hired by the end of the phone call. They were going to fly us to the plant the following week, when the salmon were predicted to start running that year.

I asked the company representative if we could just use the airplane ticket money and drive there in the van, but the rep said they had a deal worked out with the airlines. It was either fly up on their tab, or pay for it ourselves. As unnatural as it is for human beings to be airborne in a metal tube, no self-respecting hobo could pass up a free ride.

"Did they seem a little desperate to you?" I asked Lauren after we hung up.

"Desperate? No … I think maybe they were just eager to hire some very professional salmon handlers."

"Hmm."

I quit the pawn shop that day. I walked right up to my boss at the register and asked, "How much will you give me for my job?

"Huh?"

"I would like to pawn my job. How much will you give me?"

"This some sort of joke?"

"No joke. How much is my job worth?"

"Not worth a damn thing to me. What's it worth to you?" he asked.

"Not enough to keep it," I said and walked back out.

From the airplane window we could see glaciers melting down mountain tops. Looking down over those mountains, I knew that flying was a more logical choice than driving the van - more logical, but not necessarily better. I had just left and already I missed it. The majority of my adult life had been spent either in that van or with the van parked right outside. It was more or less my home and my safety blanket. Now I had separation anxiety.

"What's wrong with you, Ben?" Lauren asked me.

"Nothing. This is exciting. I'm excited."

"You're worried about your car, aren't you?" she said giggling to herself.

"It's a van," I retorted.

"Oh sorry. You're worried about your van."

"I've never been this far away from it."

"You're being ridiculous. The van will still be waiting for us when we get back. It's not going to drive off anywhere."

"You don't know my van."

"Really, Ben?"

"I'm happy I could at least bring Meal-ticket."

"Just don't worry Ben. Everything is going to be fine."

"I know. I know."

The plane landed in a town called King Salmon, where salmon was indeed king. It was one of two towns located on a peninsular piece of land that jutted into the mouth of Bristol Bay. The only ways to get there were by boat or plane, and the moment we touched down it dawned on me that we were pretty much trapped.

A pickup truck met us at the airport. The driver told us to throw our bags and ourselves in the back end to get to Brook Leader. "I'm the airport shuttle," he said with a leathery voice.

We rode down the peninsula in the bed of the truck; the majestic mountains and civilization of Anchorage a long ways behind us, and the flat peninsula and frigid Bristol Bay ahead of us. There weren't many trees around us, but there was a lot of very interesting flora growing out of the springy Alaskan tundra.

The driver leaned back and shouted through the open hatch window, "Lots of wild cotton means lots of salmon!" He smiled and gestured towards the tundra where a bunch of weird plants with stringy, cotton boll-style flowers were growing.

The truck pulled into a gravel driveway near a large warehouse building with a sign reading: "Brook Leader Fisheries; Kenkan, AK" bolted to the side of it. Not far from the warehouse was a bunch of flimsy-looking smaller buildings constructed of some kind of plywood or cardboard. We hopped out of the pickup and our airport shuttle drove off without another word to us.

"Now what?" Lauren asked me.

"I don't know. I guess we should find someone in charge."

We left our bags by one of the rickety shacks and started asking the people lounging about the property if they knew where to find a supervisor or manager or anyone to tell us what we were supposed to be doing. No one knew. Thus the tone for the job was set early.

We walked into the warehouse factory. All the big machinery was still. Apparently the salmon hadn't started running yet, or even jogging for that matter. Off we walked past the giant, silent steel machinery in search of anyone to tell us what we were doing there. Luckily, we were found by someone who seemed to know.

"What are you doing in here? What's going on?" she yelled at us.

"Ahh ... we just got here. Do you know who we're supposed to check in with?" I shouted back.

"Ohhhh. Fresh blood. Okay, well let me take your names and then I'll give you a quick little tour."

In exchange for our names, she showed us the mess hall where Brook Leader provided all our meals. There we would be fed such things as curried miscellaneous chicken parts (in all of its chartreuse glory), as well as all the fish that was deemed unfit to ship to retailers.

She showed us the company store where we were required to buy big rubber boots and rain gear in order to work in the factory. The company was kind enough to deduct the overpriced gear from our first paycheck.

Finally the supervisor showed us to our very own shanty room. "You'll be working sixteen-hour days, seven days a week once the salmon start running," she told us. "And this is where you'll most likely spend the remaining eight hours of your day." Then she walked away.

"Home sweet home," Lauren said after we'd moved all of our bags inside. Then she plopped down onto the creaky, dilapidated bed.

"Should we break our bed in proper?" I asked plopping down next to her.

After a very creaky wrestling match, I examined our little den more closely. There was a large hole in one wall from which a small electrical cord was running to our light. It was about shoulder height, and when I peeked outside, I saw a lot of bored-looking workers wandering around. I grabbed a sock and stuffed it into the big hole, to protect us from the elements and peeping coworkers or bears.

Nothing really happened for the entire first week. More new faces would arrive, and in preparation for the tedious month or two ahead of us, I started sleeping a bit more. I kept having this recurring dream. In it, my van had driven itself all the way over the mountains, through Canada, and into Alaska. It even found a way to get to the peninsula. The van and I would be rushing towards each other in a field of pristine wild cotton out on the tundra, and just before it was going to embrace me or run me over, I'd wake up.

Other than that, it was sort of like living in a modern-day Great Depression. We'd wake up early and join the grumpy crowd of would-be workers in front of the factory doors. The grumbling mass of people from all over the world would generally be complaining. "I came here to work, man."

"Yeah, I want to make some money."

Then the supervisor lady would come out and shout, "No work today!" or "Enough fish came up the fish pipe for about ten workers today!" Then she'd pick ten volunteers at random and bring them inside the plant. I was always very careful to slink away when she started picking volunteers.

Lauren laughed out loud and heckled me, "What, are you afraid of a little work?"

"No. I'm afraid of a lot of work. This job is going to be a lot of work once it gets in full swing. I just don't feel inclined to make it any harder than it needs to be. Money be damned, you can't buy sanity."

"Well what should we do with our last few sane days here in Alaska?" she asked me.

"Explore and vacation."

A kid with a knit hat who was maybe a year or two younger than me had been listening to us the whole time. He turned and asked, "You guys hitching into town today?"

"Yeah. That sounds like a good idea," Lauren said.

"It's funny," our new friend went on, "I hitched into town the other day, and the guy driving turns to me and says, 'I lost my thumb in a salmon-canning accident. You want to see it?' I figure he's just gonna show me his thumb stump or something, but he pulls this necklace out from under his shirt, and hanging on it is his shriveled old brown thumb. He said he couldn't hitchhike anymore after he lost his thumb, s'why he had to buy the truck he was driving."

I couldn't tell if this guy was full of shit or not, but I knew I liked him.

"My name's Boston Tom. Nice to meet you," he said extending his hand. "Mind if I hitch into town with you today?"

"Sounds good to me, Boston Tom," I said. "I'm Ben."

We gathered some things from our respective shacks and met back up at the highway outside the factory. The highway itself was called the Alaskan Peninsula Highway. It was fifteen miles long; the only paved road between the towns of King Salmon and Kenkan.

We stuck out our thumbs at the first pickup that came down the road, and it stopped for us. The four miles from the factory to Kenkan were spent shouting more introductions with the wind blowing through our hair. Anything seemed possible. There we were hitchhiking in Alaska. I felt like Jack Kerouac in the 1950s.

Kenkan was kind of a salmon boomtown that only came to life for a few months out of the year. There were three bars, one restaurant, a miniature library, and two sheriff's deputies roaming the streets like cowboys in a western movie. We bought a fifth of whiskey from a bar and started wandering the quiet dirt roads.

While we meandered around wooden grave markers in an Eastern Orthodox cemetery, Boston Tom told us, "I was down in New Orleans not long after Katrina hit. I got some video footage from there that you have to see. I've been working on a ... a ... well the great American documentary over the last few years. So if you ever see me filming don't pay it any mind." Then he took another snort of whiskey.

After about an hour of walking around aimlessly, drinking and avoiding deputies, we had exhausted the options of things to do in town, and hitched back to the factory in the endless Alaskan summer sun.

When we got back we found crowds of like-minded folks hanging around outside the factory living quarters, drunk and playing instruments. Guitars, mandolins, even a guitar-banjo hybrid were all being played in different little jam circles.

I ran into my shanty room and grabbed Meal-ticket, and Boston went to snag drum sticks out of his room. Then we commenced drinking and jamming like holy fools. I played 'Midnight Special,' and a rendition of '16 Tons' in which I changed the words from "16 tons" and "coal" to "16 hours" and "salmon." Boston Tom drummed along with me on a log the whole time. After we had drunk down a good portion of the fifth, I climbed onto the tin roof of a shanty and played some originals while trying to tap dance in my hiking boots. I started hearing loud cracks on and around my tin-roof stage. I looked down to see some co-workers firing bottle rockets at me, and took that as my cue to give it a rest for a little while.

There were other great musicians to be heard. The fellow on the bantar was from Turkey, and he played some beautiful, traditional-sounding Middle Eastern stuff on it.

"Did you guys all fly over here with instruments too?" I asked him.

"No. There's an abandoned house full of shit across the creek on the other side of the factory. We found these there, and just took 'em."

I found Lauren and Boston Tom chatting in a nearby circle. "We gotta go!" I shouted at them.

"What? Where?" Lauren asked, grinning at my belligerence.

"Plundering! At the nearby abandoned house!" I took another slug of whiskey. "Let's go plunder, by thunders!"

"Sure thing boss," Boston said. "Let me just round up some troops first."

He got a few of his shanty mates. One fellow knew the way, and we had a genuine search party as we passed the whiskey around.

The house was two crooked floors and a loft built from a

weird mixture of two-by-fours, plywood, and dry wall. It was dark and forbidding. Entering the hole where the door once stood was like walking into a cave. I flipped a light switch on the wall to no avail, so Boston Tom took out his video camera and turned on the camera light. The place had a definitive moldy smell and was badly trashed. We tripped over little bits of hardware and wood scattered all over the floor. Lauren and I went into a bedroom near the door. We found a dresser and an old, rotting mattress, but no instruments. I walked up the stairs with Tom while Lauren stayed to rummage through some jewelry boxes and the clothing hanging in the closet.

The second floor had a kitchen with pots and pans thrown about a smelly, old refrigerator. There was also a living room with some tattered couches, coffee tables, CDs, and mildewed books. It was eerie. I felt like a ghost haunting someone else's life, and had the urge to stay in the shadows that were more prevalent than anything else there.

"So why do you think these people just took off and left everything behind?" I asked Tom.

"I don't know, man. Maybe it was some kind of an emergency. Maybe they died in some horrific accident."

"Or," I said, "maybe they're just really messy people, and they didn't have time to fix up the place before they went on vacation ... and here we are looting their things when they could be back from vacation any minute."

I took a close look at what appeared to be a solid and growing-greenish gallon of milk on the kitchen counter. "This milk expired five years ago," I said to Tom.

"Yeah, Ben. This looks like they're on more than a vacation." He was filming a photo he had found among the wreckage and asked me, "You ever hear of squatter's rights?"

"No."

"Well apparently here in Alaska, if a house has been abandoned for more than a year, anyone who feels like it can just move in, and it's okay legally."

"Yeah Boston, I would love to move in here, but I feel like it may be a bit of a fixer-upper."

"I think the law exists to help folks survive," Boston Tom

went on, "Like if someone got lost in the wilderness and then stumbled onto an abandoned house."

I crawled up the ladder that led to a small loft, just big enough for a mattress, a bookshelf and a small closet. I poked through the closet a little bit. "Hey man, I found some sort of military uniform in the closet!" I shouted down to Tom.

"Let me see," Tom said as he climbed the ladder.

I pointed him to the closet, and grabbed a book off the little shelf by the bed. "These look like flight logs," I said as I paged through days of takeoff and landing times.

"Maybe our fellow was a pilot in the Air Force and he crashed."

I climbed down the ladder just as Lauren entered the kitchen. The rest of our search party was downstairs, yelling and crashing around.

"I found some shirts for you and some jewelry for me," Lauren said.

I grabbed a big box set of old blues CDs I had seen earlier by the stereo. "I picked us up some music," I said to her.

Lauren went through the kitchen and found a large, wooden nutcracker carved to look like a woman who cracks nuts between her legs. Just then, the rest of our search party caught up with us. One guy grabbed a rotten ketchup bottle from the fridge and sprayed on a wall in big, red, gooey letters: "I'm in the walls. HELP." Another of his friends picked up a chair and started putting holes in the other walls and busting windows.

"Let's burn the fucker down!" the guy with the ketchup yelled.

Lauren and I took our leave at that point, with Boston Tom following behind us.

"What the hell was that all about?" Lauren demanded.

"Testosterone," Boston Tom muttered.

"It's like that Graham Greene story, 'The Destructors,' where those kids tear a house apart just for the hell of it," I said.

"Should we go back and stop them?" Lauren asked us.

"I don't know if it's really our place to step in. After all, we did just loot the house ourselves," I pointed out.

"Yeah," Tom started, "but there's a lack of respect in destroying the place. Stealing is one thing, destruction is different."

"Well Boston, it's like you said, squatter's rights. That place and everything in it belongs to anyone who walks in there right now. Right now there are some angry, hormonal boys in there. They can do whatever they want," I said.

"Squatter's rights?" Lauren asked looking at me.

"It's a finders keepers law that Alaska is okay with."

"Just because something is okay by the law doesn't mean it's actually okay," Lauren said.

A slightly awkward silence followed in which the box of blues CDs in my hands started to feel very heavy. Occasionally we'd hear a drunken roar and the sound of things shattering in the house we had abandoned behind us.

I looked over at Lauren swaying with her footsteps, holding her prizes. "Nice nutcracker, Lauren."

She grinned and snapped the legs of the nutcracker together. "Thanks."

The drinking and music continued into the night, which in Alaska during the summer looks an awful lot like the morning because the sun never really sets. The fishermen had returned and were raising a ruckus on the beach around garbage can fires, smoking dope and shooting off emergency flares like fireworks.

"We're going to have the next Renaissance, man," Boston Tom slurred to me as flares went off behind him. "Me with my movies and documentaries, and you with your music and words. We need to get in a group and have a movement - overpower the forces of evil. Like the beats did in Frisco."

I just grinned and took another shot.

After a couple days, we had gotten rid of our hangovers and the salmon were running. The tender boats would stop in the bay outside the factory, and the fish were pumped up a quarter-mile pipeline from the water to the factory's holding tank. Alaska is all about their pipelines.

The holding tank was a weird sight. It was just a bunch of salmon being shot from the fish pipe into a big, concrete reservoir. The reservoir had more salmon in it than water. The guy who kept it functioning properly was the same kid who had incited the 'Destructors' episode with the ketchup in the abandoned house.

"Most all of the salmon are dead by the time they hit the tank," he told me while I was watching the strange waterfall of pink gold fall from the pipe. "But sometimes one makes it alive and starts flailing every which way. So I have to go down there with a club and beat it to death. It's awesome."

"Yeah. The job suits you."

Next, the fish went into the Fish House where they were put on a disassembly line. Their heads were first to go. A machine lovingly named "The Chink" did this quickly. It was more or less a v-shaped guillotine that got its name from the sound it made as it cut. Then workers hacked and pulled out the guts, sending the eggs to one room, the flesh to the Filet Room, and the leftovers through a garbage-disposal-style machine to be pumped back through a different pipeline to an undisclosed location in the bay, where all the bears hang out to drink salmon slurry.

In the Filet Room, the tastier parts of the fish got the final excesses sliced away, and the bones were removed by hand, one by one, with pliers. At the end of the disassembly line, the slabs of fish were graded on how healthy the meat looked, and how badly they had been manhandled. All grade A's sold for top dollar. All grade D's ended up on our plates in the mess hall.

From there the filets were stacked on racks in Packaging and Shipping and flash frozen at 40 below. They got peeled off of the freezing trays, glazed with water, and shipped out in large cardboard boxes containing 2,000-plus pounds of delicious, dead salmon flesh. Had I stolen one of those boxes and sold it by myself somehow, I would have made at least three times what I made working the season in the factory.

Lauren and I had the privilege of working in shipping. Although it was the coldest, it was the least gruesome of the jobs available. But I do remember walking through pools of blood everyday in my Extra Tuff boots, rubber overalls, and insulated gloves. Workers were divided into three sixteen-hour shifts, so that two shifts were working at all times once the fish started flowing. It seemed kind of fun initially. We were all laughing as we learned our new jobs. There was a sense of unity; a feeling that we were all going to suffer through it together. That feeling was gone by the end of the second day, when we were all ragged and ready to snap. I saw fist fights over cookies on one of my breaks. The idea of unity cost too much energy to even fake. Eventually you had to focus on your own survival.

Everyone who had complained in the beginning about not having work had now shifted gears to complaining ceaselessly about working. I probably would have complained with them, but it just seemed like a waste of energy.

We were only given eight hours of each day off. It was wise to sleep as many of those eight hours away as possible. I still tried to shower after every shift, but it seems kind of silly looking back. We'd never really be able to lose the smell of salmon on our skin until after the season ended anyway. It was in the very fibers of our clothes. Even if the laundry crew hadn't run out of detergent during the season and just started washing the workers' clothing in straight water, most of us would still have thrown out our work shirts and pants in the end. The smell was just too embedded.

Lauren quit taking showers all together. She told me, "When my hair starts threatening to dreadlock, that's when I'll take a shower." And that was fine. It seemed rational even. I quit regular showers by the end too.

I did still try to go to the meal right before my shift started every day, but most people skipped out on that too in order to maximize sleep. Breakfast wasn't exactly much to wake up to. About two thirds of the way through the season they ran out of the money allotted for bread, so we didn't get any more bread. Things just started disappearing. No more ketchup. No more Kool-Aid.

People started getting downright disgusting and weird. I flushed the toilet in one of the trailer-style bathrooms, and upon inspecting my hand I noticed poop on my fingers. Someone thought it would be funny to smear their shit onto all of the toilet levers, so people stopped flushing. I remember wading through puddles of urine to use the shower. One kid got a horrible Staph infection. Another kid got strep throat. Then we all got strep throat. At least after that, they washed our cups with soap.

We started suffering from 'The Claw.' Because we were doing the same joint-jostling motion day in and day out for sixteen hours, we'd wake up and our hands would be stiff claws that we couldn't really open or close. I'd run hot water over them every morning and rub feeling and motion back into them. I got seriously concerned for my ability to play guitar after the job ended.

"Oh buck up, Ben. The season's almost done. You'll be fine," Lauren said to me.

"I think I hate capitalism," I replied.

Obligated by contracts, we would have to pay for our flight, room, and board if we left early. The poor kid who left with the Staph infection ended up having to pay the company. The supervisors took up a collection from the workers to try and help with his bill.

There was light at the end of the pipeline though. The season couldn't last forever. As a matter of fact, ours only lasted about a month and a half.

It was dinner time in the mess hall, and I was chewing on a fish eye I had found floating in my King Salmon head soup when Tom said to me, "Could you imagine if this was a year-round job? And if people worked here their whole lives? Could you imagine what the lifers would be like?"

"No," I said. "I can't. And I won't."

One day the supervisor stepped out for a minute. We had been packing King Salmon, which is the biggest of the salmon we shipped. Without heads or innards, these frozen fish still weighed upwards of fifty pounds each. I picked up the biggest one I could find and mounted it like a horse.

"Race anyone?" I asked my coworkers.

Lauren grabbed the next biggest one, and Tom grabbed a really little one. We trotted a lap or two around the packing room, riding King Salmon that would soon be on someone's plate. Though my fish did not win the race, I believe it had the most heart.

I spent hours imagining how wonderful it would be if a bear broke into the factory. It would be like a kid in a candy store. We'd have to stop working while it wreaked havoc inside. Hopefully it would destroy all the machinery and we'd all get to go home.

One time the smokers got stuck inside during break because a brown bear was foraging through a garbage can outside the factory door. I started worrying as I walked between the bathroom and my shanty bedroom in the twilight. There I was, walking around smelling like salmon. I could feel bears watching me, and I knew they were thinking things like, 'I love me some ocean salmon, but these big, two-legged land salmon ... I just gotta get me a slice of that.'

Just when I was about to crack, the salmon slowed. They

cut our hours back. The season was on its way out, and the entire factory sighed with relief. The sense of unity returned.

I walked over to the abandoned house one more time, but instead of stealing the leftovers, I left my boots there for a future worker to use. I scrawled a message on the side of one boot that said, "Put these on and run far away from here, as fast as you can."

The day Lauren and I made our escape, Boston Tom came running like a dog after our airport shuttle as it was leaving the factory. It was like the ending scene of a movie. He caught up to the back end of the pickup and shouted, "We're going to make it happen, man! It's been a trip! I'll see you later!" The truck gained speed and he shrank in the distance, waving his arms at us on the great Alaskan Peninsula Highway.

I remember turning to Lauren and saying, "I just feel good knowing that that guy is out there doing his thing."

Lauren and I got to Anchorage with about three-and-a-half grand to put in each of our bank accounts. From Anchorage, we took a bus up to Denali National Park. We set up the tent and then we slept. We woke up and ate cheeseburgers, and then we slept again. Then we woke up and found our hands unfolding. Then we slept some more.

About six months after my tearful reunion with the van in the Lower 48, I got a call from Boston Tom. "Hey man, I was thinking about coming out to Wisconsin and moving in with you and Lauren. We could start a band and kick-start that renaissance. I looked up some Greyhound ticket prices. I could be there day after tomorrow. What do you say?"

"I don't know, Tom. There's not much room where we're living right now. The timing might not be quite right," I said.

"Wait - wait. Listen to this," he said, and then he proceeded to play 'Turn the Page' on drums, belting the whole song out through his speaker phone. He even threw in a harmonica solo. I laughed and listened, eating up all four minutes of it.

"Listen," I said after he picked the phone up again. "Maybe we can get something together but the timing isn't right for a big move right now. Give me a call in a week or so, and I'll talk it over with Lauren."

He called back about a week later, but I didn't answer. I never called him back, and I would never get another chance. A few weeks later, Boston Tom hung himself.

"There's another toll coming up," Lauren said to me from the van's navigator seat.

"Are you serious? Do we even have any more cash?" I asked her.

"No. We used it up at the last toll," she sighed. "You should go get some money from an ATM at the next gas station."

I pulled the van off I-90 and parked in front of a station. The ATM inside went ahead and charged me three dollars. My bank in turn took three more dollars out of my account as I had used a machine that wasn't the right brand. It cost six dollars to get a twenty dollar bill out of my account; all for the sake of paying the thirtieth toll that had pummeled us since Chicago on I-90.

"This is just another reason why we should never take interstates," I said to Lauren, shutting the van door hard as I climbed back in.

"We don't have much of a choice on this one, Ben. If we want to make it to Maine in time for the blueberry season, we need to go there directly. We can't putz around with our guitars and banjos on those sweet little desolate back roads. If we did, we'd arrive in Maine just in time for the blueberry harvest to end."

"What's wrong with that?" I asked.

Then we were back at it, pushing the tolled miles behind us, carving through the air in a red bullet called "Van." It was early August and the blueberry harvest was supposed to start any day up in Maine. We had no job waiting for us this time. We were going more on a whim than anything else. Lauren had gotten the name and address of a blueberry company that a professor of hers had worked at.

"He said that it's really easy to get a job up there for the blueberry season. We just have to show up. It's hard work though, real salt of the earth kind of stuff."

"It can't be any harder than a salmon season," I said.

After a night of camping with our new rummage-sale tent in Acadia National Park, we had breakfast in a Bar Harbor cafe. I took a phone book hostage and found the number to the factory that Lauren's professor had told her about. An old man answered the phone.

"Hello. You've reached Wildman's Blueberries," he said.

"Hi. My girlfriend and I are looking for work this blueberry season, and we were told you were the folks to contact."

"Well that's true," the old man said. "Wildman's is the biggest operation in the state. Why don't you come on out to the compound today and we'll see what we can't do."

"Okay. Sounds good."

We turned the van towards the town of Cherryton, also known as 'The wild blueberry capitol of the world.' A few hours crawled past as the van climbed over wooded mountains beside the Atlantic like a bug over a mossy stone.

Our destination was a little factory nestled in a pine forest just outside of Cherryton.

"Where are all the blueberry fields?" Lauren asked as we walked toward the building.

I shrugged my shoulders and we walked through a door labeled "Office." An old lady with large, square glasses sat at a desk across from the door.

"Can I help you?" she asked.

"I called earlier today about working for Wildman's, and

the fella on the phone told us to stop on by."

"Work doing what?" she asked.

"Raking blueberries," I said.

"Why I'm sorry," the old lady-secretary said. "All of our raking jobs are filled. I can, however, give you the phone numbers of a few folks who might need extra help."

"That would be helpful," Lauren said.

The secretary started writing names and numbers on a little, pink slip of paper. "You kids got your own berry rakes? It'd help your cause if you did," she said.

"No, ma'am," Lauren said. "We just drove here from Wisconsin. We've never harvested blueberries before."

"Well, we sell rakes, but they cost seventy dollars each."

"I think we'll pass on that for now," Lauren said.

The bespectacled old secretary gave me the contacts and wished the two of us luck. We thanked her, and were on our way.

The cell phone Lauren and I shared was having a hard time with reception since we had arrived in Maine. So we started driving back through the little town of Cherryton in hopes of finding a payphone to work on our new contact list.

"Seventy dollars for a rake?" I wondered aloud as I scanned the main street.

"Must be a hell of a rake," Lauren said.

"I bet it's huge. Maybe we can just split one," I suggested.

"Maybe we can just build our own with two-by-fours and TV antennas," Lauren replied.

Luckily for us, the one gas station in town had a payphone. I started making calls while Lauren cooked up a little lunch of beans on the sidewalk. We had recently purchased a propane cooker. 'Oh, if the Nashville hobos could see me now,' I thought, 'they would laugh me out of my hobo title for good.' We were rolling around in a van equipped with a propane camp stove and a semi-functional cellular phone.

The payphone only got me through to one place: The Mertil Blueberry Freezing Company. We'd have to work eight hours a day, seven days a week for five weeks in a factory freezing and packing blueberries. I started to have salmon-processing-plant flashbacks.

I told the news to Lauren as we ate lunch on the van bumper. "What do you think?" I asked her.

"Let's keep trying those contacts. I think we'd both rather work in the fields. I had my fill of factory work up in Alaska," she said.

"That's what I was thinking."

We chewed beans in silence for a few minutes.

"Ben?" Lauren asked. "What if we don't find work up here?"

A furrow of worry was spreading across her forehead like a tree's root system reaching for water.

"Worst case scenario, we don't find work. This is just a vacation then. We'll hang out at a beach for a couple days, then drive back, making music stops to cover gas." The worried root system on her forehead started retreating. "Hell," I went on, "that may even be the best case scenario."

She rolled her eyes and said, "Let's go back to that campground by Bar Harbor."

We were tent-ridden that evening as a thunderstorm rolled over us. Our night was composed of a bottle of wine, a deck of cards, and a Crazy Eights tournament.

By morning the storms had passed and we went into Bar Harbor where the cell phone had reception. I started working my way down the pink contact list again. This time I got through to Buck Mills of Mill-Time Organic Farms. He told us to drive up to the farm that afternoon so we could chat in person.

Two hours of highway brought us to a dirt road that weaved through cattle and chicken by a dairy barn. The road curved up to a house that doubled as Mill-Time's office. A slender lady only a few years older than Lauren answered the door.

"Hi. We're supposed to meet Buck here about blueberry raking jobs," I said.

"Ohhh. Come on in, I'm Buck's daughter, Michelle."

We waited on a sofa in the front room while Michelle tried to call her father. After a few attempts, she sat down on the sofa next to us. "So where are you two from?" she asked.

And that got Lauren and I launched into the story of where we were from, how we met, what we did, and what we were doing in Maine. It was always fun to recite this story to folks we were meeting, but it was starting to feel almost like a routine: A comedy or storytelling skit where both Lauren and I had certain punch lines about our lives and adventures that we said at certain times.

It was strange because sometimes in these introductions, I'd start to feel like an actor who was only acting out the role of myself. Maybe it was more like a sales pitch in that particular case: "Look at what we've done and/or are doing! Like us! Hire us!"

After our routine ended to the silent applause of our minds, Michelle started telling us about herself and how she was born into the organic family farm.

"My first memories are of learning how to milk the cows, and being chased around the yard by roosters," she said. "It's been hard work, but I feel better for having been raised this way."

Then she started talking blueberries. "You'll basically put in as many hours as you feel like, and work as hard as you feel like. You don't get paid for your time; you get paid for the quantity you pick. But if you want to make it pay off at all, you'll be working pretty hard," she said.

"How much will we get paid?" Lauren asked.

Michelle pondered a moment and replied, "I'm not sure how much it will be, but I promise you, it's the going rates."

"Also," I interjected slowly, "we don't have rakes yet. Could we possibly rent a pair or something?"

"Ohh," Michele laughed, standing up. "I bet we have some rakes lying around that you could just borrow for the season. I'll go get a couple."

As Michelle walked into the garage, her mom walked out of what appeared to be an office with a slip of paper in her hand.

"You two are so polite," she said to me and Lauren. I think this actually took us both a little off-guard. We had been called many things between the two of us before. Polite was a new one. "You kids are unfamiliar with blueberry raking, but it's sort of a tradition here in Maine. Let me read you a poem Michelle wrote when she was nine."

It was a cute little blueberry blues poem, and it was actually pretty advanced for a nine year old. As she read it, the somewhat absurd and naive notion entered my head that this blueberry job was similar to the cotton field work that a lot of the old bluesmen of the Mississippi Delta had done. Maybe I'd find some musical inspiration in the work, or somehow become a better musician.

"What did you think?" Mrs. Mills asked after she finished.

"That's better than I can write now, and I'm a songwriter," I said.

"Yeah, that's my daughter. She's a talented girl."

Michelle walked back in from the garage with two big, metal hand rakes. "Mom!" she exclaimed, grimacing when she saw her mom standing next to us with the poem in her hands. "Tell me you didn't read that blueberry poem to them."

"I did. And they liked it," she said and marched back into the office.

"She's always reading that thing. Sometimes I wish I hadn't written it," Michelle mumbled as she handed us each a hand rake.

"I think it's sweet," Lauren said as I studied the hand rake.

The rakes were about a foot and a half wide and made entirely of a strong, lightweight aluminum. The handle faced the same way as seventy-two thin, cylindrical prongs. These prongs were close enough together that blueberries would not slip through, and they each came to a dull point to cut into the blueberry bushes. The prongs and handle were connected to a box-like area at the end of the rake. In effect, the actual raking of blueberries was more like scooping them off of their plants and into the collection box at the back end of the rake.

Buck, the boss man, made his appearance soon after we

got the rakes. He barged through the front door and started to rush around the office and kitchen like a cheetah on
speed. "We need more pickers. Why isn't Don here yet?" he
mumbled to himself while frantically digging through stacks
of papers.

"Slow down. You're going to give yourself a heart attack,"
Michelle said to him. "You got some new rakers right here."

Buck did slow down long enough for a glass of water and
asked, "You're the couple I talked to earlier today on the
phone?"

"Yup."

"Great. Welcome aboard. If you got a tent, you can camp
on the fields if you like. There's an outhouse out there too.
The pay is twenty-two cents per pound." Buck guzzled his
glass of water. "Sorry to run like this, but I gotta get the tractor jack back on. Michelle, call Don and find out where he is."

And then he was gone out the front door again. It was the
easiest job interview I've ever had.

Michelle went to the phone and her mother called us into
the cluttered office.

"Here are the directions to the fields," she said. "Just fill
out this paperwork and show up there at eight o'clock in
three days."

I could see Lauren doing the math in her head as we drove
out of the farm.

"We'll need to pick about five hundred pounds to get one
hundred dollars," she stated.

"Is that good or bad?" I asked.

"I don't know. It kind of sounds bad though."

"It's the going rates."

That night at the Bar Harbor camp was a misty one, so
again we had no campfire. Instead we sat in the tent, plotting
and debating under the warm, electric glow of the flashlight.

"I don't think I want to camp in the fields," Lauren said.

"Why not?"

"It's probably going to be in the middle of nowhere, and I

want to be near real bathrooms and civilization."

"Maybe there's civilization near the fields. Let's research the place tomorrow morning."

"Okay."

We fell asleep as the mists of Maine soaked through everything and made the arthritic joints of the trees creak in the night.

We packed away our dripping camp gear the next morning, and fired up Lauren's laptop in a motel parking lot.
The motel offered free Wi-Fi so we parked and took it. I discovered that the town the fields were in - Meddybemps - indeed had no civilization in it. Nor were there any other towns near Meddybemps. Lauren was eating a peanut butter sandwich while I searched.

"Whelp," I started, "there is nothing in Meddybemps. It is literally the middle of nowhere. So I looked for campgrounds and the closest one I could find is in Stanley, which is a forty-five minute drive from the fields."

"Well forty-five minutes is closer than this Bar Harbor campground, isn't it? Let's give it a shot," she replied and smacked some peanut butter in her mouth.

"You know, though," I started in again, hoping to change her mind, "I heard that it's a really easy commute to work when you camp on the fields. And every night you can eat fresh blueberries until you shit blue. Which I think is pretty neat. Not to mention how little it costs to camp there. It's a good deal."

"Yes, but I heard that all the men who camp there get dumped by their girlfriends," she said and smiled at me sweetly with peanut butter on her cheek.

Two-and-a-half hours later, we were driving into Stanley. We cased the town and found it well-equipped with a grocery store, gas station, and a few restaurants.

"Is this civilized enough for you?" I asked Lauren.

"There's no Ikea, but this will have to do," she said sarcastically. "Where's the campground?"

The campground was on the outskirts of the other side of town. It was well overgrown. The sign was unhinged, but it did say "Open." I went and knocked on the office door while Lauren waited in the van.

"Come in!" a gruff voice shouted in reply.

I walked in to find a man in his late forties, with about three days' beard growth, wearing dirty overalls, and leaning back in a chair with his muddy boots on a cluttered desk.

"Hi," I said. "We're looking for a place to stay for the extent of the blueberry season."

"Really?" he asked as he clomped his muddy boots onto the floor and leaned forward in his chair. "You must be workin' the fields?"

I nodded and caught a whiff of a whiskey-based cologne he must have been wearing.

"Well, I usually charge twenty-two a night. But if you stay for an extended time, we can work out a fifteen dollar-per night deal," he said, mumbling a little near the end.

"Okay, let me run it past the lady," I said and walked outside to the van which doubled as a conference room that afternoon.

"This place gives me the creeps," Lauren said. "How come there's no one else here? Where are we supposed to camp if everything is this overgrown?"

I may have been starting to get cranky. "This is just the entrance. You're the one who didn't want to camp on the fields. The next closest campground is another hour away."

She sighed and looked hard at me, and I continued, "The guy said he would give us a seven-dollar discount per night if we stayed the blueberry season. Let's drive through it and see what it's like, okay?"

We drove down the grassy road, located a shower house, and a bathroom with running water. There was only one site occupied, but there didn't seem to be anyone in or around the tents. I pulled back around to the front office shack where the office man was standing outside.

"I don't want to stay here," Lauren said as we sat in the van.

"Well where are we supposed to stay for the season then? I feel like we should try and figure this out before the harvest starts. You don't want to stay in the fields, we can't afford motels, and this is the closest campground. There are other people here. I'm sure this place will be fine."

"This place just sort of gives me the shivers."

I touched her arm. "Let's just try it for a night or two. If we get comfortable, we'll stay. Otherwise, we'll figure something else out."

"Okay. Okay, fine."

I was overly confident that this would be the place. I really wanted it to be. I wanted to stop having to worry about it, and let all our damp camping gear get a chance to dry out.

I got out of the van and explained to the man, "We're just going to try it out for a couple nights. But the fields are forty-five minutes away. We might find something closer yet."

"Okay. Sounds good. Let's ring you up."

I followed his sour-mash aroma back into the office. He sat down behind the desk and I fished out my credit card.

"My cat, George," the man said, "he got runned over by a semi, on this very highway out front of the campground."

I handed him my card and said, "I'm sorry to hear that."

He took a good look at my card and said, "He was the best mouser in the state. I'd wake up every morning and there'd be a dead mouse by my shoes, sometimes two. Sometimes he'd put 'em in my shoes. One time he even brought me a rabbit, and we e't 'im up for dinner." He swiped my card.

"You have a lot of mice around here?" I asked.

"No. No, George took care of that. Now he's dead. Golly I miss him."

He tore off the receipt and handed it over with a pen for me to sign.

"When did it happen?" I asked

"About ten, no ... twelve years ago now."

I slowly looked up at him to see he had tears in his eyes.

"I'm really sorry to hear that," I said. I looked back down

again and saw that I had already signed the receipt. I handed it over to him.

"Camp anywhere you like," he said, looking at the receipt with a big grin.

We set the tent up in a spot not too far away from where the other tents were set up. Then I took a nap in the afternoon sun as our gear dried from the past two rainy nights. After a propane-cooked dinner of couscous, I said to Lauren, "You know, we're both kind of filthy right now. We should take a shower."

"Right now?" she asked, and pivoted away from me. She was wearing very short khaki shorts. One side was pulled halfway up a round ass cheek and she hadn't noticed. I had.

"Yes. Now. Right now," I said.

Lauren looked confusedly over her shoulder at me, saw where I was looking, and caught the drift. "Oh. I see we have the campground to ourselves ..."

"Um-hmm," I said standing up and gathering our towels and some shampoo.

"We can do whatever we want," she said and smiled wickedly.

I was standing next to her, licking the salt off her neck, with the fixings of a good shower under my arm. She reached over and grabbed me by the crotch of my jeans.

"Let's go take a shower," she said and gently pulled me by my crotch to the shower house.

We were getting snuggled into our sleeping bag for a well-earned nights sleep. I was just about to say something to the effect of, "See Lauren, this place isn't so bad," when the neighbors showed up.

Arriving in a cavalcade of muddy pickup trucks, they got out, started screaming incoherently, laughing uproariously, and blaring metal music. I looked over at Lauren and saw her reaching for a flask of whiskey.

At about 3 AM, I was ready to go over and politely ask if they could quiet down. When I was about to leave the tent, one of them started talking loudly about his prison time and knife fights. Unfortunately all my knives were hidden in the van somewhere, so I lied back down next to Lauren and tried to force myself to sleep. She had finished all the whiskey, and was actually managing some semblance of sleep.

I heard the vehicles leave at about five in the morning, and finally got a few hours of rest. Lauren was staring at me when I woke up.

"You still think this is the place to stay?" she asked me.

"Maybe the noisy neighbors will move on today," I sleepily said.

"Hmmpf," Lauren replied as I tried to jump back to sleep.

We were driving into town for brunch when we passed the fellow from the office. He waved us down.

"Well what do ya think?" he asked as I rolled my window down.

"It was all right," I said. "But the other campers were a bit rowdy."

A lightning streak of a frown crossed his face. "Those are some of the locals," he said. "They camp here a lot. You might wanna get a spot further away from them."

"Will do," I said and started driving again.

"Let's get a spot in a different campground," Lauren said to me.

"How about on the blueberry fields?" I asked.

She actually thought about it for a moment this time, but came out with the same results. "No, I want a bathroom. And I want people nearby."

"You want or need?" I asked.

"Shut up," Lauren said.

After brunch, we came back only to find the locals had started partying early that day.

"Can we please leave?" Lauren asked.

"We could," I said. "But we paid for two nights." I was still convinced that this would be the place we were going to have to settle for. "Let's just move the tent."

After the gear had been thrown into the van and the stakes had been pulled, Lauren drove to the site furthest from the locals and nearest to the highway.

"For a quick getaway," she said as she parked the van.

We were reset in the new spot, and I was sitting on a stump strumming my guitar when the office man walked up to us and asked, "How ya doing?"

"Pretty good, just trying out a new spot," I said.

"Good, good. You two make yourselves right at home. Drink, smoke, go skinny dipping in the river, take a shower together, whatever you want."

It seemed like he had begun partying early that day too, and the fact that he mentioned "shower together" sort of weirded me out. I managed a smile, and looked over to see Lauren peeking out of the tent at us, her eyes shining in the dimness with a confused, piercing look.

Then the camp host continued talking. "See, you're adults. But little Dolly Parton ..." at this point he pretended to grab large breasts on his own chest, "lil' Dolly Parton, she's only eleven and can't be drunkin' or smokin'. You folks do whatever you like though ... and don't think I'll be spying on you or nothing."

That pretty much sealed the deal. We were going to have to leave. "Gee. Thanks," I said to him.

"No problem. Now excuse me, I'm going to go start a wire fire," he said and turned to leave.

"What?" I asked.

"Oh. I got all these old power lines lying around here. They got copper in 'em which is worth quite a lot of cash these days, but I can't trade 'em in with the plastic coating on them. So I'm just going to burn that shit off." He started walking away from us, further into the campground, but turned and added, "If the smoke from the fire gets too bad for ya, you might want to move your campsite." Then he disappeared down a trail.

Lauren walked out of the tent and stood next to me. Her

arms were crossed, she was grinding her toes in the dirt, and the look on her face nearly knocked me off the tree stump.

"All right. We'll leave," I said stifling laughter.

The very next day at the ass crack of dawn, we packed everything up and made our getaway to Meddybemps for our first day of work. As we had arrived quite early on that foggy morning, I decided to take a nap. When I woke up it was past eight, and there was only one other vehicle there, a black SUV. Lauren had been reading the whole time.

"Is boss man Buck in the SUV?" I asked her.

She looked up from her book and said, "I'm not sure, but I don't think so."

"I'm going to go check it out," I said, rubbing my eyes.

I walked up to the driver's side window with Lauren following behind me, and saw that it wasn't Buck in the SUV, but a muscular Mexican man, his wife, and two children. The man rolled his window down. "Is Buck here yet?" I asked him.

He shook his head and shrugged his shoulders like he didn't know. The window right behind his rolled down and a six-year-old girl poked her head out and said, "No. Buck is not here. He must be late."

"You all doing the raking?" I asked.

"Yes we all are," the little girl said.

"So are we. This is Lauren, and I'm Ben," I said.

"Hi! I'm Jenny Gomez, and this is my older brother Bryan Gomez," she said gesturing to the boy in the seat next to her. "And that is Papa Gomez and Mama Gomez." The man in the front seat nodded as Jenny went on. "They don't speak English, so Bryan and I translate."

"Well it's nice to meet you," Lauren said, and we shuffled back to the van.

Fifteen minutes later, several more vehicles had shown up and parked around us. None of them were Buck. The Maine sunshine was starting to burn some of the fog off so we could more clearly see the surroundings. The blueberry fields were a vast low-grown green carpet that spread over the hills and jagged rocks of an ancient, decaying mountain range. Because of the rocks and uneven terrain, hand rakers were needed. Otherwise, our jobs could have been done much quicker with a machine. After every harvest season these blueberry fields went through a controlled burn in order to put nutrients back into the earth for the next generation. Due to the biannual burns, the berry plants never grew much higher than ankle height, hence the nickname "Lowbush blueberries."

We saw the Gomez children burst out of the SUV and start eating blueberries and tossing rocks back and forth. Lauren and I got out and started having a blueberry breakfast too.

"We should call him," Lauren said.

To my surprise the cell phone had a little bit of reception and just enough battery power to accomplish this task. Buck answered with a gruff, sleepy voice. "Huh? What? Hello?"

"Ahh ... hi Buck. This is Ben, one of your blueberry rakers. We're out at the fields like you told us to be. What should we do?"

"Oh yeah. That's right. I'll be over there in twenty minutes or so," and he hung up.

Then we played our own little telephone game. I told Lauren what Buck had said, and Lauren told Bryan Gomez, who told his sister, who translated it to their parents.

Half an hour later, Buck pulled up in a half-sized semi (a semi-semi), and started pulling big, square five-gallon plastic bins out of the trailer. He would hand a stack to one of his helpers who would disperse the piles along the road at the edge of the fields. I went over and helped move the bins as Lauren grabbed our rakes out of the van.

Another car parked nearby during this process. It was a fancy little Mercedes that had mud all over it from the dirt road. A man in a suit got out with an adolescent boy dressed like he was about to play a baseball game in the Thirties. They came over to the semi-trailer and started chatting with Buck. Lauren went over and they introduced themselves to her. I caught little snatches of the conversation as I unloaded bins.

The man in the suit was saying, "It's a rite of passage, and anyway I think little Ty could use the money, right Ty?"

Ty, his son, looked at him and nodded blankly. I overheard Lauren breaking into the introduction routine without me.

"From Wisconsin, huh? And you don't have any place to stay?" I heard the man in the suit say. "I don't suppose you could take Ty to his mom's house after the work day is done here? It's only twenty miles away ..."

I stopped with the bins and walked over to see what Lauren was roping us into.

"You must be the musician," the businessman said extending his hand.

"I guess so," I shook his hand.

"I'm Brad, and this is my son, Ty."

I looked down at Ty who was standing a little behind his dad. The look on his face said that he would have rather been anywhere but there.

Brad continued, "I was just talking to Lauren here, and she mentioned that you two don't have a place to stay tonight."

I cut in a little, "Well, we got a tent. And the van. We were thinking we might just camp on the blueberry fields tonight."

"Actually," Lauren broke in, "Brad was telling me about a little inexpensive motel not far from here. We've been camping in the rain and cold for the last week or so. Maybe we could stay at the motel and get a good night's sleep tonight, seeing as it is our first day of work and all."

"Okay. I guess."

"And seeing as Ty's mother's house is on the way, do you think you could drop him off after work is done?" Brad asked us.

"Sure," I said.

Brad drove away, shooting a trail of mud and gravel behind him.

Vacation ended and the work began. The fields had been divided in approximately equal rows sectioned off with strings that stretched from one end of the field to the other.

These rows between the string boundaries are referred to as ricks. Every blueberry picker or picking group chooses the first available rick and picks it clean, then moves down the line to the next available rick. All the berries that get raked up are dumped into the plastic five-gallon bins. When a bin is filled nearly to the brim, it gets stacked on the roadside at the end of the rick and is tagged with a piece of paper and the name of the raker. From there the bins get picked up and Buck records the tags and numbers in a pay book.

"Twenty-two cents a pound is how much I'm paying," he said as we put on some gloves and hats, "which means you'll be getting five dollars for every five-gallon bin you fill."

Some ricks were packed with berries. Others barely had any. Either way the ricks needed to be picked. There were a lot of huckleberries growing around and within the blueberry fields too. It's very tough to tell these two berries apart when you are moving quickly. We all ended up just raking them along with the blueberries.

"It won't really matter anyway," Buck explained. "There's a lot more blues than hucks. And anyway, this is all going to be processed and made into pie filling, so no one will know the difference."

Though we had already figured it out, Buck came up to us, grabbed a rake and demonstrated the 'proper' raking method. He bent down, pushed the seventy-two metal prongs near the bottom of the ankle-high bushes, and the ripe berries fell off into the collection area of the rake as he scooped it forward and up.

"That's all there is to it," he said. "Now get in a rick and pick."

Lauren and I got a rick two down from the Gomez's, with a different picker between us. Ty got the one on our other side.

"So how old are you?" I asked Ty over the rick line as I made the first scoop of the thousands that would follow.

"I'm thirteen. How old are you?"

"Twenty-five."

"Wow," he responded spitting out a blueberry. "And look how well you've done for yourself." He laughed sarcastically.

Oh, I could tell this Ty was going to be a real charmer.

As we got further into our first ricks, the rest of the fog lifted, and our shoes took on a dewy moisture that they would keep for the rest of the season. The shoes I brought to work with were re-gifted to me from a friend. He was a star volleyball player and had received them as a gift. Unfortunately for him, they didn't fit properly. Fortunately, they fit my giant feet, so he just let me keep them. I was picking blueberries in style, in a pair of never-worn Nike Air Jordans. The shoes actually cost more than I could rake in blueberries during a day.

"I don't want to rake anymore," Ty yelled over to us.

"Well as far as I understand, we can pick as little or as much as we want, but we get paid for how much we pick," Lauren said back to him. "So if you need a break, go for it."

He sat down and started putting gobs of the berries he had just picked into his mouth.

I turned and added in a bogus-fatherly way, "Keep in mind though Ty, the season is just starting. If you need a break already and you haven't filled one bin yet, you may be in for a long season."

Ty rolled his eyes at me as Lauren and I continued down our rick. We eventually filled our first five-gallon bin, and dragged it to the roadside to tag. It wasn't until we finished picking our first rick that I saw Ty get up and start raking again.

It was very peaceful backbreaking work. I'd eat a few berries now and then and stand up to admire the scenery as I wiped berry juice off my chin. The Gomez family moved fairly quickly from rick to rick leaving us far behind. The children waved at us and shouted "Hello" every time they went past. After eight or so hours of raking and fifteen bins of berries filled between Lauren and me, my back was giving me the signal that it was quitting time.

"My mom is an art teacher. My dad is a businessman," Ty told us on the ride to his mother's house. "One time two summers ago, my dad took me to a Yankees game. It was awesome. I'm going to be a baseball player. I'm going to try out next year in high school. It's going to be awesome."

"What kind of business does your dad do?" Lauren asked him.

"You know. Business. Businessman business," Ty replied as though Lauren had asked something really stupid.

He pointed us in the direction of the motel when we dropped him off.

The Rainbow Rooms Motel was composed of two trailer houses shoved end to end and painted bright pink. It cost $40 for a night there.

"That's over half of what we made in the field today," I mentioned.

"Who cares?" Lauren asked. "That means we're still coming out ahead. Aren't you happy to be out of the tent and the van and in a real building with real privacy?"

"Not especially."

The color theme of the room we checked into was green ... sea foam green. The walls and the furniture were all painted sea foam green, even the almost-clean sheets were sea foam green. The room smelled a little bit fishy and rotten, like a New Jersey beach.

"This color is a ballsy choice for a room," I said as I set Meal-ticket onto the raggedy, slanting brown carpet.

"Yeah, not many places can pull it off," Lauren chimed in happily.

"I sort of want to see what the other rooms look like. If each one is sea foam green or if they each have a different color theme."

"It's the Rainbow Rooms Motel, Ben. A motel this wonderful would not limit itself to just sea foam green," Lauren said.

I thought it was funny because a few weeks earlier, this motel room would not have been up to Lauren's standards, despite its very charming color.

When I went to take a shower, I was surprised to find that even the shower had a thick coat of sea-foam-green mildew. The only mismatched item was the towel with the big blood stain on it. The maid had probably forgotten to place this towel in the red room.

After showering, I walked out to find Lauren in bed drinking beer and watching "Full House" on TV.

"Now this is living," she said to me.

I couldn't help but laugh and hopped into bed next to her.

We slowly checked out at seven-ish in the morning and drove back to Meddybemps for the next round of back breaking.

"I'm giving up on finding us a permanent base camp for this job," I said to Lauren. "I guess we're just going to have to figure it out one day at a time."

When we got to the fields, we found Ty and his dad waiting for us.

"Hey you two!" Brad yelled as we got out of the van. "You still looking for a place to stay?"

"Yup," I said.

"Well I'll make you a deal," he said getting into business mode. "If you two pick up Ty in the morning and drop him off back at his mother's when the work day is done, I'll let you stay at my dad's cabin for free."

This sounded too good to be true. "Where is it?" I asked.

"It's about thirty miles from here on Lichen Lake."

This sounded promising. It sounded like we might have found a perfect compromise between mine and Lauren's different living standards.

"I gotta warn you," he went on, "there isn't any electricity or water. But we have a couple ten-gallon tanks we can bring for water, and there is a gas stove and gas powered lights."

All right so it wasn't quite perfect. But it was close. "Count me in," I said. "What do you think Lauren?"

"Okay," she mumbled and looked away.

"Great!" Brad said. "I'll show you the way when you drop off Ty tonight." Then Brad zipped off to do whatever business it was that he did in some other parallel universe.

I sat down on the van bumper and pulled my soggy Air Jordans on. Lauren threw a pair of gloves at me and we each grabbed a rake and headed to the next rick. Ty waited back and then went to the rick right after ours. It was apparent that he would be tagging along with us throughout the season.

"It's really cool, what your dad is doing for us," I said to Ty over the rick line.

"Yeah. He's like that. He can be awesome when he wants," Ty said.

"What's this cabin place like?" Lauren asked him.

"It's all right. It's my grandpa's. I don't go out there much because there aren't any video games."

I started into raking and noticed I was moving much slower than the day before. My back was stiff. My arms were stiff. Even after my muscles loosened up, they never stopped aching. By the end of the day, both Lauren and I were visibly fighting collapse every time we bent down to scoop up berries. I started cracking up at the sight of us, and we called it a day.

On the ride to Ty's mother's house, both Lauren and I were drained from the fields. Ty was lively as ever. Lauren was trying to keep up a conversation with him, but I wasn't really even there. I was just trying to focus on driving. We had a good deal worked out with this cabin, and I didn't want to ruin it by getting us all killed in a car accident. I followed the conversation as well as I could, but all I really heard was Ty saying how "awesome" everything was every other sentence. Sometimes it seems that kids are like solar panels, but instead of absorbing and making energy from the sun, they absorb and use the energy of adults.

We pulled into the driveway, and Ty darted into his mother's house.

Brad walked out of the house and shouted "Follow me!" He got into a pickup truck and we followed him down the road.

I started testing the water with Lauren as she hadn't said another word about the cabin since the morning. "We really got a break, being offered these rustic accommodations," I said.

"Yeah," Lauren said.

The paved road stopped and turned to gravel. This gravel road cut through a forest and by a few random cabins along the edge of Lichen Lake.

"Do you think it's strange?" Lauren asked.

"What?"

"These people don't even know us, and they invited us to stay in their cabin."

"Well. We're doing them a favor with Ty. Now it's almost like they're sending him off to a bad summer camp through us," I said.

"It doesn't strike you as weird that we're following a total stranger into the middle of nowhere?"

"Brad isn't a total stranger. You know he's good people. And actually he's putting a lot of faith in us, trusting us with his son and all. And how does he know we won't ransack and burn this cabin down? Because he knows we're good people too," I reasoned. "Also, I don't think he likes getting his car dirty when he drops Ty off."

Lauren picked up the cell phone as we drove further down the gravel road. "Phone has no reception here," she said dropping it down on the floor between the seats.

"Quit with the paranoia already," I said.

After creeping along eight more miles of gravelly, pine-forest road, Brad turned down a side dirt road. It twisted its way to a little, picturesque log cabin that overlooked Lichen Lake with the evening sun beating on it.

I helped drag the water containers out of the pickup and into the kitchen with Brad. It was a musty-smelling place, in the tradition of most old cabins. The main room acted as a family and dining room as well as kitchen. The feature that really stuck out was the giant portrait window that looked down on the lake. Out that window, I saw the sun falling and shattering into thousands of pieces on the waves.

"All right," Brad said. "Quick tour. Only drink the water from these tanks," he said pointing to the two ten-gallon tanks we had just dragged in. "Here's the long-stem lighter.

You will need that to start the lanterns and the stove. The room on the left is my father's room. You'll be staying in the kids' room to the right." I peered into our room and saw that it was just big enough to fit a bunk bed and a single bed.

"As you can see," Brad continued, "there is a bathroom between those two rooms. It does not work. Don't use it. You can use the pit toilet in the outhouse that we passed by the driveway. There's a canoe over by the shore, feel free to use that if you want. Any questions?"

I looked over to Lauren to see how she was reacting. She shrugged her shoulders silently.

"All right, just pick Ty up in the morning at about seven thirty and bring him back when the day is done. Here's my number, call if you have any questions," Brad said handing over his card. "Enjoy!" Then he was off again.

I looked at his card after he left. "Hey Lauren, turns out Brad's business is wedding planning."

"Really?" she asked. "He must be a good one."

"Maybe he thinks he can make clients out of us," I said and laughed out loud. Lauren didn't seem to find it funny.

Grabbing the last couple of beers from the van, I walked into the little cabin and gave one to Lauren.

"This place gives me the willies," she said cracking her beer open.

"This place is beautiful. I think we just walked back in time to a little slice of paradise."

"Paradise is creepy," Lauren said and chugged her beer.

In the distance, I heard the mournful call of a loon. It sounded like every Hank Williams song being played at the same time and then smoothed out.

We woke early enough to pick up Ty and get to the fields around eight. Thus the routine began. We'd chat with the Gomez children a little bit when we got there, put on our rotten gear and fall into the rhythm.

On that third day we worked the stiffness in our backs out rather quickly, maybe a side effect of sleeping on mattresses for two nights. We picked thirty bins worth of berries, which was the best haul we had made.

I remember pausing in the middle of my rick on top of a big rock, eating a handful of berries, and staring out across the pines. I saw fish jumping in a pond between the blueberry hills. I could hear Jenny Gomez singing in Spanish a few ricks away from me.

Then I felt something sting the back of my neck. When I turned, something hit my chest. I looked up and something hit my cheek.

"Ty!" I shouted. "Quit chucking blueberries!"

"If I'm going to be an awesome pitcher for the Yankees, I gotta practice."

"Your mind is in the wrong field, buddy. We pick blueberries in blueberry fields. We throw baseballs in baseball fields," I said.

At this he took a handful out of his bin and threw all of them at me at once.

"Ty! Don't be a jerk," I shouted. It was taking some willpower to not start throwing blueberries back and let the whole day devolve into a miniature blueberry paintball match. You couldn't really blame him though. He was a thirteen year old being a thirteen year old.

When Lauren and I got back to the cabin that night, we pillaged the cabinets and found a bottle of rum and some cigarillos. A drunken canoe ride ensued followed by a shower in the shallows after the canoe tipped over. I grabbed the shampoo and soap and we made the frigid, clear water of Lichen Lake our bathtub. What we didn't know, and Lauren for some reason would find out repeatedly, was that Lichen Lake had leeches.

I was drying off on the porch and getting ready to cook some food when I heard Lauren screaming bloody murder. I looked up to see her just standing on the shore and screaming at her ankle.

Sprinting down the porch to the shore, I asked, "What's wrong?"

"Leech!" she yelled, and pointed at her ankle. "Get it off! GET IT OFF!"

I bent down, looked at her ankle, and saw the slimy little culprit.

"Yup," I said. "It's a leech."

"I know it's a leech. And it's sucking my blood. Get it off!"

"Should I get salt or something and sprinkle it on the thing like a slug or just pull ..."

"Just get rid of it!"

I picked the little leech up by its slimy tail and yanked it lightly but it was not letting go. It just pulled her skin out with its sucker.

"It's definitely drinking your blood," I said.

"BEN!"

"All right, all right." I gave it a hard yank and the leech popped off Lauren's ankle. "It's gone now," I said and tossed the vampire worm into the bushes. I stood up and wrapped a towel around her.

The rhythm of the season continued. We'd pick Ty up in the morning, work the fields, and drop him off. One day while we were working, two big, white vans showed up. Out of them came about twenty new workers, which nearly doubled the work force Buck had on these fields.

"They were flown in from Haiti by a different farm," Buck told me, "but that farm hasn't started harvesting yet, so I contracted them until the other farm starts."

When I walked past the newbies, I couldn't help but notice that my Air Jordan work shoes were raising eyebrows and getting strange attention. 'Yes I am wearing these hundred-and-fifty-dollar shoes for a blueberry harvest,' I imagined myself telling them. 'You should see my good pair (which was a ratty, old pair of flip flops).' Then I started to worry that maybe Nike had a factory or something in Haiti.

Maybe some of my new coworkers were personally familiar with my work shoes.

Only one fellow among them seemed to speak English. He acted as a crew boss of sorts. All he ever said to me was, "Nice shoes, boy."

I don't know if Buck thought he was falling behind with the rakers, but he didn't have to worry about it when the new workers arrived. They were fast. They were professional. They could pick two-and-a-half ricks before Lauren and I could pick one. The season was growing shorter.

"My mom and the Gomez's are working on some music together," Ty said to me one evening on the ride to his mother's place.

"Really?"

"Yeah. I told her that you're a musician too, and they're hoping you two could stop by for dinner and have a jam thing tonight."

"How does your mom know the Gomez's?" Lauren asked.

"They're staying in my mom's garage apartment for the blueberry season," he said.

"Oh?" I asked. "Do your folks just put up blueberry workers who need a place to stay all the time?"

"Well not every year, but a lot of the time."

The seemingly random generosity of Brad started to make more sense to me now. 'They're nice people,' I realized. 'This is just what they do.'

"Dinner and a jam session sounds nice," Lauren said.

"Yeah, I'm in," I added.

I hadn't really had much of a chance to play on this East Coast excursion and I was worried that my hobo-musician stylings might be a little rusty. With Meal-ticket in hand, I followed Ty and Lauren into the house.

Ty's mom was sitting at a piano with a ukulele in her hands. She was in her mid-forties, had short, salt-and-pepper hair and wore a pair of John Lennon-esque eye glasses. Across from her was a sofa where the Gomez kids were sitting.

"Hello, you two travelers. I'm Ty's mom, Susan. I've heard a lot about you."

"Hi," Lauren and I said in awkward unison.

"Listen to what we are working on!" Jenny Gomez said excitedly, jumping up and running over to Susan's side with Bryan at her heels.

Susan grinned and strummed the uke. Jenny and Bryan started belting away traditional Mexican folk songs as loudly as possible. Without any inhibitions, these two kids sang with visible joy on their faces. It spread from the little singers to Susan, and then permeated the entire room in warm waves. Lauren and Ty and I were all smiling and clapping in time by the end of the first song, and without stopping they moved onto the next.

"En la cantina!" they closed the second song, waved their arms and took a bow as we clapped loudly.

"More! Encore!" Lauren cheered.

"I'm afraid that's all the music I've learned with these two so far," Susan explained.

"We're hoping to perform at an open mic next week," Bryan said excitedly.

"You play us a song now," Susan urged me.

I played a short set of some silly originals mixed in with some traveling songs. Susan and the kids were enjoying it, but Lauren seemed kind of restless. After I finished, I gave them each a CD.

Then Jenny said, "My parents are making comida, let's go eat."

We feasted on tacos with homemade tortillas that night. Bryan had popped a Pixar movie into the DVD player. It was in Spanish, so he spent the whole evening translating the movie for Lauren and me. There is something in a child's perspective, something whole and limitless that we lose when we become adults. I kept hoping he might translate that to us as well.

There were a few rain days when we didn't go to the

fields or only worked a partial day, and then it seemed like the ricks were almost empty.

"Let's just cut and run," Lauren said after another half day. "I want to go home."

We packed and left the cabin in a scramble and made a round to Ty's parents' and the Gomez's place to say goodbye. Brad and Ty were gone, so we left thank-you notes for both of them with Susan. Susan sent us off with a fresh peanut butter pie and a sealed yellow envelope that she had written "Because I believe in you ..." on.

Setting the envelope aside for the moment, we drove off to the Mill-Time headquarters to return the rakes and work out the financial end. Buck gave us a $1400 advance for the few weeks we spent working there.

I turned the van back towards Wisconsin, but pulled off at a wayside not far from Mill-Time.

"What's up?" Lauren asked.

"I just gotta take care of something." I gently took the rotten Air Jordans out of the van. They reeked of foot, sea-foam-green mold, and biohazard. I dropped them into a trashcan at the wayside, and then ran back to the still-running van. With tires squealing, we hit the road again. I expected that the garbage can would blow up soon after I had dropped the shoes in.

Meanwhile, Lauren, sitting in her copilot seat, had picked up the yellow envelope and opened it.

"Ben?"

"Hmmm?"

"Susan gave us a hundred dollar bill."

"Really?"

"Yes," Lauren said pulling it out and waving it at me.

"Well those people are just ridiculously nice," I said.

"What should we do with it?" Lauren asked.

We both stared down the misty highway that we were chasing down.

"Let's go to Bar Harbor," I said. "Get some fresh lobster and go on that brewery tour."

And that's exactly what we did.

1,200 miles later, we were driving on a backwards little highway in Gary, Indiana. I had played at a few bars and diners along the way without much luck. I was still hoping for one more big score before we got back to Wisconsin.

At the happiest of hours, I parked the van by a dilapidated bar. It looked like the roof might be caving in. It also looked like happy hour had skipped over Lauren.

"What?" I asked her.

"First off, we just got paid for the blueberry season. We have enough money to get back. Why do you keep stopping to play?"

"Because ... that's what I do."

She rolled her eyes. "And secondly, why do you choose to play the most run-down bars you can find, in the most dangerous-looking neighborhoods?"

"Because they need music the most. And anyway, people with a lot of money don't seem to tip nearly as well as the customers in joints like this."

Grabbing Meal-ticket, I asked, "Are you coming in this time?"

She started shaking her head, and then opened her door and stepped out. "This is the last one, Ben."

The smoky little bar only had about nine or so people in it. I introduced Lauren as my wife, and gave the bar sales pitch.

"Yeah sure," the gray haired matron running the show said. "You can play."

I opened the guitar case and played some old-time country and blues music. This was Gary, Indiana, and I thought some working-man songs were in order. I made thirty-five dollars in thirty minutes, ten of which came from a confused, drunk woman who may or may not have realized that she tipped me twice.

The first time, she was stumbling past me towards the bathroom. She stopped to ask, "Where are you traveling to?"

"Back to Wisconsin," I said.

"Good. Get as far away from here as you can," she said and dropped a five spot in the guitar case.

Ten minutes later, she came out of the bathroom and

asked between songs, "Where are you traveling to?"

"Wisconsin," I said again.

"I hope you get there," she said and dropped another five dollar bill into the guitar case.

"You too," I blankly said as she tripped out the front door.

I wanted to stay longer and try to wring more money out of the crowd and meet the new folks coming in, but after thirty minutes, Lauren was making it clear that she wanted to leave. She was off at one end of the bar, avoiding the locals at all costs, and motioning to me to wrap it up. After putting Meal-ticket back in its guitar case home, I walked over to the bar.

"What's up?" I asked.

"I want to leave," she said.

"Is it okay if I get a beer first? I'm thirsty."

"Yeah, I guess. Make it quick."

Two drunk men walked over to us. They didn't give me any tip, but the older one said to me, "You're all right, but you should sing 'Bad Moon Rising' in a deeper voice, 'cause when you sing it, it sounds like you've been kicked in the balls," and then he laughed loudly while his younger friend just sort of leered at me and Lauren ... mostly Lauren.

The older one gave me his same critique of 'Bad Moon Rising' two more consecutive times and cracked up after each go as if it were the first time he had said it. Someone at the other end of the bar was trying to flag me down, and sensing an album-selling opportunity, I went over, leaving Lauren to deal with the two weirdos. She's tough. I figured she could handle them.

While I was raising a couple more dollars, those two guys were apparently telling Lauren every horror story they could think of - all the urban legends, bad movie plots, and news headlines about unsuspecting folks traveling on the road meeting terrible ends. The older fellow questioned Lauren about whether she carried a weapon, and then to demonstrate what he meant he flashed a piece.

By the time we left, they had talked her into a mess. She was crying as we drove away.

"What's wrong?" I asked.

"Those two guys at the bar told me awful things," she said between sobs. "Awful people. I want to go home."

I pulled off the road and hugged her. She sobbed into my shoulder, "I would have stayed in the car by myself, but I was scared because it looked like a bad neighborhood."

"It's okay," I said rubbing her back. "Those guys were drunk assholes. Had I known what they were doing, I would have told them off."

"No. It's not okay!" she shouted pounding her fist into my back.

I let go, backed up, and just looked at her. Tears were still streaming down her cheeks.

"I don't want this anymore," she confessed. "I want to live in one place. A nice safe place. I want a career and a family."

Her sobbing was becoming more regular as she regained control of herself. I looked out the windshield at the road that lay straight ahead.

"I can't promise you any of that," I said.

"I know," she said. "I know."

The home front was falling apart. Lauren had grown or changed in our time together. Maybe she had always been that way, and thought that I would come around to her side of things after we had traveled a bit. She wanted stability, security, and comfort. She wanted a house, a career, and a family. Maybe she thought I needed to get this 'hobo bug' out of my system; that it was like a virus. The truth of the matter was that the 'hobo bug' was my system. I didn't want stability, security, comfort, or convention. Those were almost dirty words to me. Those were the traps that people threw their passions away for.

I didn't know exactly what she was thinking, and I couldn't really ask her. A wall of silence had been growing between us, getting larger with each passing day. I was still living with her in the efficiency, and sort of fell back into my old routines outside of our personal life. I became the anchored-down hobo, playing gigs in order to scrape up half the rent.

I was scouring Craigslist one day, trying to find music work and more venues when I came across an ad seeking lounge musicians to play on cruise ships. I answered it. The next day I got a request for ten thirty-second video clips of me playing music. They specifically asked for cover songs, saying that originals would not apply.

'What the hell,' I thought. 'What have I got to lose?'

I filmed the song bits on Lauren's laptop camera while she was at work and sent them to the cruise agency in the morning. By the time Lauren got back from work that day, I had already received an answer.

"Guess what?" I asked her when she walked through the door.

"What?" she answered evidently annoyed at my having broken our unspoken code of silence.

"You know how you wanted me to get a 'real' job with a potential career?"

"Yes."

"I just landed a corporate job."

"What?" she inquired, looking up at me quickly with eyes that wanted to smile but were waiting for a catch.

"I'm going to be working for Festival Cruise Lines."

"Doing what?" she asked.

"As a lounge singer. I answered an ad on Craigslist."

"Really?" The spark of happiness in her eyes fizzled out.

"Yup. The agency I'm going through is legit too. I checked the Better Business Bureau website."

She hung up her jacket. "When do you start?"

"In a month. They gave me the choice between a three or six-month contract, but the agency is really pushing the six-month one."

"Six months where?"

"On a cruise ship. All over the Atlantic. I would live and work in a floating city." I couldn't help but smile. At the beginning of the day I had no idea if I would even be able to pay for another tank of gas to get to the next gig.

"You actually want to do this?" she asked looking searchingly at me.

"Yeah, why not?"

"Of course you would."

Of course I did. It would be one of the better tricks I could pull. I'd be kind of a reverse hobo. Instead of traveling around to little towns and suburbs to bring music to the people, the people would come to me with each new cruise.

"You're the one who wanted me a get a steady job," I pointed out.

"When I said that we should both start considering some

solid careers to help us settle down, being a lounge singer wasn't exactly what I had in mind."

"It's a corporate gig. It even has a retirement package if I stay with the company long enough."

"Yes, but if you work there you'll be homeless, except for whatever boat you're on. Basically nothing will change besides a boat taking the place of your van. You'll still be a hobo. Just a corporate one."

"Corporate hobo?"

"Well in this case a water tramp, a propeller tramp, a pirate-hobo, or sinking singer or whatever falsely-romantic name you want to pin on it." She turned and went into the bathroom, shut the door and shouted through it, "Well congratulations! It sounds like it will be really good for you."

I went to Lauren's computer and confirmed six months at the job. The agency purchased and e-mailed me a plane ticket to Miami for the beginning of the next month.

Lauren and I fell back into our routine of silence. January passed in slow, glacial movements. The heater in the house didn't work right, and there was no more love between us to keep warm either. The day of my departure crept up and Lauren drove me to the airport.

"Well ..." I said standing outside the terminal.

"Yep." She agreed to nothing at all.

"So this is how we end?"

"I'm thinking so."

"What no song this time?" I asked, grinning.

She punched me in the shoulder and then looked up at me. "I don't want to hold you back from what you want. You don't want to hold me back from what I want. That's all there is to it."

I looked into her face and saw the same woman from the Wyoming bar that got me blackout drunk and more or less stole my van, kidnapping me with it. I saw the same woman I worked an eternity with in salmon processing plants and in blueberry fields. I saw the same woman I could barely even speak to anymore.

"I agree," I said.

She squeezed me next to her in a final embrace, and I kissed her forehead.

"I love you," I said, and walked out of her life.

As the airplane flew towards Miami, I thought about the ridiculousness of what was actually happening. They had asked for a list of 200 songs that I knew how to play. I knew barely half that many. So I just made up the last hundred, figuring I'd learn them as I went. I could have just as easily faked the entire list and sent video clips of ten songs that I had learned specifically for the video, and still gotten a free ride to Miami. How were they supposed to know? I hadn't signed any contracts yet. I was still under no obligation other than my word. Had I really liked Miami, I could have jumped ship before I even boarded.

I wanted this gig though. So even though I was selling my soul in a way, I was going to follow through - D.B. Rouse: Hobo-Sellout.

After landing, I took a cab to the Port of Miami, filled out a cornucopia of paperwork, and walked onto the big, white, floating island I was to call home for the next six months. This particular Festival cruise ship could hold 3,500 passengers and 2,000 crew members. I began dragging my bags and guitar into the intestinal depths of the ship, then stopped and watched other crew members passing by. As I wondered what I should do next, one crew member approached me. He was wearing a nametag that said: "J.D. - Music Director." He had thick, square, Malcolm X-style glasses, a crew cut, a thin mustache, and was carrying a manila folder. He glanced at my guitar and said, "You must be my new lounge singer."

"I must be indeed," I answered him.

"Follow me with your bags," he said with an air of boredom.

J.D. navigated through a labyrinth of halls to a destination unknown. All I was focused on was keeping my bags with me, and making sure I didn't run into one of the sprinkler heads that randomly dotted the hall ceilings. The halls were rather short, and being a rather tall, lanky man, I could have easily bumped my head on a sprinkler and set the whole ship's fire system off. That would have been a great first day on the job.

"This is you," J.D. said, handing me a keycard and pointing at a door. I slid the keycard into the lock and walked into my new room. It was about the size of a closet and a half; just enough space for a small desk, a narrow bunk bed, and a personal bathroom that would barely fit an ironing board.

"You're lucky you're a soloist," J.D. said. "It's written into your contract that you get your own room. I have to share mine with another show band member."

I dragged my bags into the room and set them by the bunk bed, successfully taking up all the open floor space. J.D. was waiting in the hall, watching with arms crossed and foot tapping.

"Come along now," he urged. "I'll show you the mess hall and your stage. I'll give you a map of the ship in a little bit, and you can figure out the rest on your own."

He took me back into the maze of crew-member-only hallways and backdoors. I felt like a test-lab ship rat following the leader to a kilo of cheese. He opened a door and took us into the main lobby area, the wide open atrium of the boat. In the center of our floor, framing glass elevators in a 'C' shape was the atrium bar. Inside of this C shape, behind the bartenders was a stage with a PA system and a grand piano.

"That's your stage," J.D. said.

Then he took a little pin out of his pocket and handed it to me. It had the same design as his, except mine said: "David - Lounge Singer." They went with my first name. It felt strange, since no one had ever called me by my first name. I'd always been D.B. or Ben.

"All employees must wear the mark of the Festival beast at all times on board," he said. I poked the pin into my T-shirt, and he went on. "Also, there are certain bars that crew members are not allowed to sit at. The bar staff will cue you." He started flipping through his folder. "It's a big ship at first," he said handing me a map, "but I'm sure you will be feeling claustrophobic in no time."

Then he handed me a schedule. I looked at it and noticed I was supposed to play a four-hour set that night. "It says I play four hours tonight," I said.

"Yes?"

"But it's my first day. I thought maybe I'd have a night off to get adjusted to the ship."

"Think again. You're not on vacation. This is a job. Your first shift is tonight."

"Okay."

"Also, as long as we are on the topic of vacations and rules, I feel it's especially important to tell you musicians that if you get caught fraternizing with the guests romantically, you will be terminated immediately. Have all the sex you want with crew members, there is a giant box of condoms in the laundry room. But guests are off limits."

I nodded. He glanced at his watch and said, "Have someone else show you the mess hall. I have to get to show band rehearsal. Welcome to Festival."

He walked off in a hurry and I took a closer look at the PA system and my stage. There were no cords or microphones there. That would be an issue. I looked above the stage and saw the ceiling was ten stories up. The hallways on the guestroom floors above all had overlooks aimed at the atrium bar and my stage. I could conceivably be heard by ten floors of people at once. Behind the stage, the back sides of two glass-case elevators moved up and down ceaselessly, giving passengers a ten-story interior view of the ship.

I made my way back to my room, and was surprised to not get lost. Between shaving and putting on a tuxedo that I was required to buy for the job, I took a closer look at the schedule. It was a six-day work week. Four days were to be four-hour sets; two would be five-and-a-half hours long. How was I supposed to stretch the hundred songs I barely knew into even three hours? I was going to have to play every song I knew every day; some of them twice. I would have to throw in some originals too. If they had a problem with my doing originals, I'd just say it was an obscure Woody Guthrie song. I sat at my desk and started working on a set list for the night.

I nodded off in the chair briefly until a mechanical, tornado-like whirl woke me up as the engines kicked off and the propellers got into gear. Like a hedonistic torpedo of pleasure, we shot out of the Miami harbor for a seven-day cruise to Ocho Rios, San Juan, and Cozumel. I shot out of my room and navigated my way through the bowels of the ship up to the atrium bar stage.

A man with the mark of the beast was waiting on stage when I got there. His tag said: "Chris - Audio Technician."

"You must be David," he said.

I glanced down at my nametag pinned through my tux vest. 'David, that's right,' I remembered.

"Yup," I said looking back up at him.

"Welcome aboard. I'll be helping you get your sound set up. I'll also be the guy you should come to if any of the gear starts acting up. My office is at the back of the cigar bar."

"Thanks," I said. "Good to know."

"All right," he said bending down next to the PA mixing head located beneath the grand piano. "This is a pretty simple system. We'll put your microphone in channel one, your tracks in channel two, and guitar in input three. Where's your mic?"

"Don't have one," I said.

"That's okay, we've got a whole bunch of them in storage. I'll go grab one. Cords too?"

"I need those too."

"You going to need me to sing for you too?" he joked.

"No, but would you tell me what the tracks are that I'm supposed to put in channel two? I might need those."

He started laughing at first, but then quickly turned serious when he saw that I was serious. "You don't know what tracks are?"

"Nope." I had opened my guitar case to start tuning.

"But you're a soloist. You must have backup tracks. You know ... tracks to back you up."

"Backup tracks of what?"

"A pre-recorded band. Drums, bass, guitar, piano, and everything... usually MIDI files. It's sort of the industry standard on cruise ships"

"What is this karaoke? Am I supposed to be a rapper or something? I have my guitar," I stated bluntly.

"Well this ought to be interesting," he sort of mumbled. "Sit tight, I'll go get your mic."

I gazed out across the lounge at the few tables of scattered people and the couples at the bar. I looked at the folks in line at the nearby help desk. I looked up to see a child peeking down at me over the eighth-floor railing, took a breath, and took a smile.

About ten minutes later, my audio technician rushed back to the stage edge, handed over an expensive microphone, and said, "This will be your microphone for the extent of your contract. You are responsible to bring it wherever you're playing. If you lose it, it will be docked from your paycheck. Return it to whoever is working the audio department when your contract is up, okay?"

Before I could answer, he hopped up on stage, and started plugging in cords and handing me the other ends saying, "Start playing. I'll make adjustments as you go."

I opened the first set of my seafaring career with 'Dock of the Bay.' Chris had me sounding pretty good by the end of it and left as a smattering of applause came in.

"Be nice to me folks, it's my first day," I said and started belting out the next song.

By the end of the second night, I was starting to lose my voice. I ran into J.D., my music director/boss man at the midnight buffet in the crew mess hall.

"How you holding up, David?"

I stared at him blankly until I realized he was talking to me; that my cruise name was still indeed David. "Oh ..." I said and coughed, "okay. I think I'm losing my voice though."

J.D. looked at me, deadpan. "I know, mate. I listened to you sing last night. You're good, but you gotta pace yourself. You're here for six months, right?"

I nodded.

"You won't last a week if you keep at it the way you are. I've seen it happen to lots of folks. This is no time to burn out. You must learn to fade away like the rest of us. Understand?"

It dawned on me that I would have to reprioritize. It would no longer be all about giving a strong, passionate performance. It would now be about surviving. I started to pull back more and more at each show/shift. I developed new, lazy and careless performance habits for the sake of surviving, putting forth less and less effort so as not to wear myself out. It worked in the sense that I was able to continue performing on the ship's rigorous schedule, but it would take me years to unlearn the bad habits I developed for the sake of surviving.

"Take tomorrow off," J.D. told me.

After a good twelve-hour nap, I rose to the next day with exploring on my mind. I grabbed the map J.D. had given me, and went back to the atrium bar. Instead of going to my stage, I went one floor up a half-spiral staircase to the stores and balconies around the atrium. There was a sunglasses shop, a tourist trinket shop, and a duty-free liquor store. Festival photographers were hard at work right outside the store doors on the balcony, taking pictures of guests in front of big, fake-tropical backgrounds.

I stood next to a guest who was watching the same thing, and asked him, "We're going to islands in the Caribbean. Why don't folks just wait to get their pictures with real backgrounds?"

"Oh. It's just something to do," the fellow said.

I couldn't argue with that. There was no visible staircase to the next floor, which was apparently where the guest rooms began, so I wandered down a large hall into the next spectacle on that level. The hall opened wide into a noisy casino. There was a little stage located pretty much on the side wall of the hallway, midway through the casino. It was more or less a large, glorified step. On this step, a larger fellow with an electric guitar strapped to himself was about to start playing. I felt bad for him. The only seats for folks to watch him were right in front of slot machines, and his audience seemed to be paying more attention to the slots than him. He walked over to the mixer, picked up an iPod that was plugged into the system, and walked back to his chair where he had a stand with a music book on it. After he noodled with the iPod a bit, a cheesy-sounding, synthetic band started playing through the speakers. These must have been the mysterious "tracks!" It was hard to hear at times because the din and racket of the slots and gambling tables were so loud, but the soloist was doing a karaoke-meets-Guitar Hero rendition of 'Brown Eyed Girl.'

'That's funny,' I thought to myself. 'I play that song too. Maybe I should stop because he plays it.'

Further down the hall I walked past an empty piano bar, a beatboxing disco, and into a nostalgically stinky cigar bar. A duo was performing Caribbean music there. With the industry-standard tracks backing them, they played steel drums and sang. They were in the middle of a nice rendition of 'No Woman, No Cry' when I walked in.

'You gotta be kidding me,' I thought to myself. 'I play this song too.'

Feeling wary about the short song list I knew, I took the stairs up to the top-most deck and stepped outside. There were four different pools, a giant screen for movies, a water slide, a track, and a driving range. There was also a stage where a country band was playing. I was relieved to hear that it wasn't one of the songs I knew. While I was staring off at the infinitely distant ocean horizon, the country band finished one song and started another. It was 'Folsom Prison Blues.'

I couldn't believe it. Every song in my small repertoire was already being played to death. No one was ever going to listen to me at my bar.

I began walking back to my cabin, hell-bent on learning new material. I stopped at the tenth-floor overlook and braving vertigo, leaned over the railing to see my stage down below. 'If anyone throws anything at me from this height, I hope it'll at least be in the form of a large bill,' I told myself.

'Pennies would hurt more than just my ego from here.'

When I passed through the casino again, I caught the musician there playing the end of 'Folsom Prison Blues.' I started laughing. 'Who gives a shit?' it occurred to me. 'I'll throw in originals when I can, but it doesn't really matter. We're all playing the same things here. It's like live radio.'

While attempting to learn some new music in my cabin, I heard a horrible grinding sound coming from the engine, and the general motion of the boat slowed to a halt. After several dings and whistles over the ship intercom, the head-honcho voice of the cruise director came on and said, "It's a beautiful day here at Ocho Rios, Jamaica! We'll be in port for the next four hours so go have an adventure!"

New songs could wait. This propeller tramp wanted to see if his land legs still worked, and see another country besides. My land legs led me through security, off the ship and into the heat of Ocho Rios.

The first thing you may notice upon entering Ocho Rios is that everything in town is surrounded by military style, razor wire-topped fences. It's these little touches that can really bring out the charm of a slum. The people living there are friendly in a desperate and pushy fashion. And why shouldn't they be? Coming fresh off a cruise ship, every one of us tourists smells like money.

The locals like to step directly in front of you, forcing you to stop so they can make friendly offers: "Do you need a taxi?" or "Do you want your hair braided?" With so many friendly locals, it's actually kind of tough to walk anywhere.

One fellow stopped me and put out his hand to shake mine, so I offered mine as well. "Do you like flea markets?" he asked me.

Who doesn't like flea markets once in a while? "Yes," I said, and the mistake had been made.

"Follow me," he said.

We traveled three blocks as he led me to a fenced-in flea market. Traveling with this fellow leading was much easier and quicker because he was literally shooing other town folks away from me, quietly telling them, "He's mine." When he wasn't shooing people away from me, he was trying his best to be like a tour guide. "See that mansion way up on the hill over there?" he said in an accent dripping of Jamaica. "That's Keith Richards' mansion."

Once at the market, he took me directly to a tent in the middle. "This is my sistah's place," he said, and his sister waved at me from a chair by the tent. "She has the best stuff."

I glanced at the tent next to hers and saw that they seemed to be peddling the exact same things. "No, no. This tent," he said, grabbing me and pulling me inside.

'Well I do need gifts for the folks back home,' I thought to myself, and I started inspecting the wares. But every time I paused to look at something, his sister would pick up whatever it was and put it in my hands. Keychains, necklaces, mugs, and more all went into my hands as the proprietress offered me a deal of some sort.

"You can have four mugs for twenty dollars," she said.

I'd smile, shake my head no, and set the items back down. I really just wanted to make a getaway, but I felt obligated to buy something. So I bought a five-dollar shot glass that said "Jamaica." She actually seemed angry at me for only buying one, after she had gone through the trouble of putting four shot glasses in my hands.

My tour guide, observant fellow that he was, could tell that I wanted out of there. After my shot glass purchase he said, "Follow me," and I followed him back out of the fenced-in market, past outstretched hands trying to stop me, shouting that I must see their special set of uniform crap for sale.

"You said you were hungry?" my guide asked me when we were standing back on the street.

"No. But I am actually hungry. What's Jamaican cuisine like?"

"I know just the place. Follow me."

We walked another three blocks as he explained, "We're going to a place that everyone in Ocho Rios goes to. A very good place."

It wasn't until we had gone through the door that I realized we were in a Jamaican equivalent of a KFC: a KFC without any health codes or apparent standards of cleanliness.

"I don't think I want to eat here," I said. "Actually I know I don't. I'll be on my way."

I walked back out the door with my tour guide at my heels. He tapped me on the shoulder and I turned around. His mood seemed to have changed. There was a dark cloud coming over his face. "You know," he said, "normally people pay twenty dollahs for this sort of thing."

"What?" I asked, finally understanding what I should have understood to begin with. "Twenty dollars for a scary man to take me to a fast food restaurant?"

He glared at me and stuck out his hand.

"Fine," I said and handed him a five dollar bill.

"Not enough," he said, accentuating every syllable.

I handed him two more dollars, turned around, and started walking back to the ship, dodging beggars left and right, almost like I was in some sort of horrible old video game. One old man with glazed-over eyes stopped me by the boat. "What's ya lucky numbah?" he asked me in a weathered voice.

"Nine," I said.

"Listen," the old man said, seeming to drop whatever act or pitch he had prepared and just being human. "I am an old man. And I am very hungry. Could you spare two dollahs for a necklace I made out of coffee beans?"

I gave him two dollars, put on the necklace and finished the Jamaica level of the video game.

Later on, J.D. would say, "Yeah, no one goes into Ocho if they can help it. It gets better the further you get out of town. Do a land tour through the cruise ship next time. Or you could just pay the fifteen dollars to go to that fenced-in beach on the other side of town. Beggars rarely get in there."

The days sailed by like space ships to the moon. I learned and refined my new singing-to-survive strategy. I'd still give my all once in a while; usually for my originals, which I would only play when I had a friendly or particularly attentive audience. One day I looked out at the bar and saw a woman was sitting alone, watching me, and crying. I was playing one of my love songs called 'Swimming in It.' It was the first time that I had caused a lady to cry without having done something wrong. I was confused. My learned reaction in such moments was to ask, "What's wrong?" or apologize and promise never to do whatever it was I had done again. I finished the song and watched her blow her nose and wipe her eyes.

"I'm sorry," I mumbled into the mic. "I won't do it again?"

I grabbed a CD and handed it to the bartender to hand to her. The lady handed a note to the bartender to give to me. The note had her room number on it.

A few days later, J.D. sat next to me during lunch. "Word's gone 'round to the cruise director," he said.

"Oh? What's that?"

"You've been selling CDs in your lounge."

"Ohhhh. That. Yup, it's true."

"You work for the corporation. Festival doesn't like people to make money off of them if they can't get a chunk or benefit from it."

"So festival is going to take a percentage of every five-dollar CD sale I make?"

"No. The only rule and requirement regarding the selling of CDs is that you have written a song about Festival Cruise Lines, and that that song is on the CD."

"Really? Does it have to be a positive song?"

"Yes."

"Like a jingle or what?"

"Almost anything really. You just have to give Festival Cruise Lines a loving, promotional, artistic nod."

"What if I stop selling them and just start giving CDs away?"

"As far as I know no jingle is needed for that," he said.

"All right. It's settled," I said.

So began a great self-promotional strategy: the sampler CD. I'd burn a handful of songs onto a disc and put it in a paper sleeve with a business card and information on where to purchase full-length albums. It was like the old drug dealer strategy. The first few songs are free, but once you're hooked, you gotta pay for the rest. I'd hand the CD out to folks who tipped or went out of their way to say nice things. So when a fellow gave me a fifty dollar tip in cruise ship poker chips and a shot of Patron tequila from the bar, I gave him a sampler CD. When I saw a lady singing along with me to an obscure Townes Van Zandt song, I gave her a sampler CD. When a man said, "You sound a lot better than the guy who was playing here last night," even though I was the guy who was playing there last night, I gave him a sampler CD.

For the first three months I was genuinely, albeit carefully, enjoying myself. While most of the employees who worked on board in housekeeping or bartending or both were working twelve-hour days, I was only working four or five hours. I fell into a glorious routine of sleeping at least ten hours a day, waking up and walking around the track, reading, writing, recording, wandering around Cozumel and San Juan, and playing music.

Occasionally I'd go to the crew bar in the depths of the ship, get a cheap drink and try to socialize. At first I hung out at the table with the Americans and Canadians. All the entertainment jobs were filled by the people sitting at this table. We all had it pretty easy compared to the other workers. Our work was playing music. The show band sometimes had a work day that consisted of fifteen minutes of playing. The weird part about this table was that its inhabitants could not stop complaining. They complained about how miserable working on a cruise ship was and wished they were home. I could see their point to a certain degree, but the more I hung out with them, the worse things seemed. They were picking scabs, poking at loose teeth with their tongues, and only making things worse. Every time I saw them they would recite a litany of complaints with new words. In the end this ceaseless complaining was a trap. Things stayed complain-able, because they kept complaining about things. I think the bottom line I took from that group was that anyone can have a bad time anywhere. Sometimes it takes effort to have a good time. But it's usually worth the effort. Over time I've found that the best reaction to almost anything is to laugh at it.

Folks at a table in the corner of the crew bar were always laughing. I was drawn to them. One night I walked past the entertainers and sat with the corner table. "Hi. I'm D.B., David actually," I said looking down at my nametag.

"Yes. I've heard you play in the bar. I work as a photographer a floor above you. I am Dersead, but you may call me Doug," the guy at the end of the table said to me with a slight Eastern European accent. "I've been moving up the ranks," he continued. "Photography is better than housekeeping. But I know there is a job on board somewhere that involves very little work and responsibility. I am looking for that job."

'You should try being in the show band,' I thought to myself.

"I'm from Serbia," Doug said. "Where in America are you from?"

"I'm from Wisconsin. We have lots of cheese."

This gave rise to a few chuckles, and a man next to Doug who had been munching on food pushed a plastic bag my way and said, "I'm from Mexico City. We have lots of grasshoppers." There was more laughter as he motioned me to dig into the bag and have a bite.

The bag was filled with dried and salted grasshoppers. I picked a couple out and inspected them as the rest of the table watched in smiling silence. The hoppers were very delicate, and very dead. They hopped into my mouth and I crunched down on them.

"What do you think?" the Mexican man asked.

"They're good. Kind of like sunflower seeds. Sunflower seeds that taste the way grass smells when it's just been mowed," I said and pulled a bug leg out from between my teeth.

I thanked them for the snack and bought a round of beer. As the night wore on, it became apparent how much they liked their jobs. "We work here many hours a day. But we work on this fantastic ship," Doug said, "with internet, a clean place to live and shower. Back home, it is tough to find work. My parents and family live in a very rundown place. I send them most of my money."

The fact that I had been complaining along with the rest of the entertainment table earlier made me feel spoiled rotten. I tried to make a conscious effort to complain less after meeting them. Many drinks later, and I was carefully stumbling to my cabin on a ship that would not sit still. After getting into bed, I remember telling myself I would just close my eyes for a moment and then brush my teeth, but as the ship rocked on the ocean waves, I fell asleep.

I woke up and my light was still on. Stranger yet, I was in the top bunk. I had the room to myself and I always slept in the bottom. 'How drunk was I?' I asked myself. 'What? Did I have an accident in the bottom bunk?'

I peeked over the bedside at the bottom bunk and saw the headstock and neck of my Meal-ticket resting on the pillow, with the blanket tucked gently around the rest of it.

At some point, everything about the entire cruise line job started to blur into itself. Every day was starting to seem the same. Even the tourists boarding with each new cruise seemed exactly the same. Everything was becoming a big glob of plain mashed potatoes. I was still surviving, but I was getting ragged. Summer approached in a blaze of monotony, until the ship changed its home port from Miami to New York City. We were switching routes for the warm months and would now be sailing from New York to St. John's and Halifax.

I got off the ship to check out St. John's. It's a quirky little Canadian town with lots of lobster and a big river that flows backwards at high tide. There was a seafood, craft, and farmers market in the center of town. On the misty days we had there, I liked to wander past the old book shops and little restaurants that made up the downtown of this old sea port. I was immediately drawn into a little record shop on a back street, and the attractive employee behind the register kept me coming back. She had dark hair, violet-blue eyes, and a certain grace in her movements as she changed records on the stereo and restocked shelves. The record shop was the first place I'd go whenever we got into port. She'd show me new music she had been listening to, and would occasionally talk me into buying a CD from her.

Eventually she told me that she was a musician too. On the next trip into town, I brought Meal-ticket. I played a few goofy songs to her from between racks of CDs and records, hoping my awkward charm might somehow win her over.

After I finished she looked smugly at me, crinkled her nose and asked, "Can I try?"

I handed over Meal-ticket, and she played a couple very slow, cryptic songs. There was a haunting ache in her voice.

I think a voice is like a fingerprint to an ear. Everyone's voice is individually unique. Somehow, the voice carries and retains bits of personal history from the singer's life. If ears could read a voice like eyes reading a palm, they would not see the future, but hear a history. She had a voice that could have sung any random sequence of words and stir emotions out of a stone.

A customer came in as she finished playing, and she went back behind her counter.

"You want a lobster roll for lunch?" I asked her.

"Sure," she said.

I left Meal-ticket in the shop and headed over to the market with her melancholic melodies still echoing in my head. I paused and looked into a live lobster tank at a seafood stand. I saw all those claws and legs and antennae struggling for space in the overcrowded aquarium. There was a very large lobster back in the far corner from me. Being taller than average myself, I could sort of empathize with it. Its googly eyes stared over at me. Then it started moving, climbing over the living landscape to the top of the lobster heap. It was still looking at me. It crossed the waters at the top of the tank, came to the corner I was standing at, and poked one of its big, rubber-banded claws out of the water, effectively pointing in my direction. I looked behind me. No one else was around. It was pointing at me.

"How much for that big one?" I asked the man behind the counter, but really, who could put a dollar value on a life?

"Twenty dollars," he said.

"I'll take it."

As the vender grabbed my lobster and put it in a box, I fished a twenty dollar bill out of my pocket. My cruise director, the head boss of the ship, just so happened to see this and walked up behind me.

"What are you doing with that lobster?" He startled me.

"Ah ... um ..."

"You know you can't take that back to the ship. You going to have a campfire and eat it here?"

"No," I said, "you don't understand. I didn't choose this lobster. It chose me."

"What?"

"I'm going to set it free."

He laughed out loud and patted me on the back. "You are something else, David."

I got my lobster box and quickly walked out of the market towards the mouth of the St. John's River and its brackish waters. When I got to the end of the longest dock I could find, I took the still-moving lobster out.

"All right big fella. You're off that cruise of doom tank ship. I'm setting you free." I pulled the rubber bands from its claw hands, and dropped it into the murky water. It sank tail first, with its claws stretched up to me. It sank like Leonardo DiCaprio at the end of Titanic.

'Maybe it's just in shock,' I thought. 'Maybe it's dead.'

I got up, brushed my knees off, and looked down into the water. It had sunk out of sight. "Quit being so dramatic!" I yelled into the water.

If it did die, it died free.

I went back to the market and rewarded myself with lobster rolls, which I took back and shared with my favorite record store worker in all of downtown St. John's.

On really stormy nights, when the boat shook and shimmied so much that it was hard to walk a straight line, most of the guests would stay in their rooms, seasick. Those were the nights that I'd play 'The Wreck of the Edmund Fitzgerald' to the staff and the few people that did come out. I'd play a half-hearted set and watch drinks slide from one side of the bar to the other. The shows continued in my lounge, and my odds of vocal survival were dwindling. Warming up wasn't cutting it anymore. I could literally feel my vocal cords swelling up. I'd have nightmares that my throat had swollen shut and I'd wake up in a panic because I thought I was suffocating. So I decided to go to the doctor's office on board and see what my free employee health care was all about.

"Well," the doctor said, "your vocal cords are swollen, and I can see that your wrist is swollen too. You must be a right-handed guitar player?"

I looked down at my big, dead-fish-limp left wrist. It was true. It was sore.

"What you really need is rest," he went on. "But as you know, I'm a doctor for Festival Cruise Lines, and I have to keep that in account as well. What the cruise line really needs is for you to finish your contract."

"Can I at least take a day or two off?"

"Sure. I'm also going to prescribe you cortisone pills for your voice and an arthritis medicine for your wrist."

"Okay."

"Tell me something though, David, have you ever considered lip-syncing?"

"Lip-syncing?"

"Yeah. On a day you feel like your vocal cords are up to it, say at the end of these next couple days you have off, you could go record vocal tracks in the audio technician's office, and then just pretend to sing on stage until your contract is up."

"Do people actually do that?"

"Sometimes."

"I don't work with tracks. It would be impossible to line my guitar and the vocals up. Also kind of on principle, lip-syncing will not work for me."

"Well you can always try scotch. That helps me when I'm trying to sing," the doctor said.

"Alcohol isn't good for vocal cords, dries them out. Scotch probably helps you more with your inhibitions than with your voice."

There was an awkward silence as we stared at each other for a moment, he with a dumb-looking smile, and I trying to figure if this guy was a real doctor or not.

"Well," he said, "I'll go get your medicine."

There was about a month to go on my contract. My voice was still falling apart, but with the meds, it was falling apart at a slower rate. Every night I'd pop my pills and then prop myself up on stage like a scarecrow. One night I fell asleep on stage. There weren't many people at the bar that night. My eyelids were getting heavier and heavier and my guitar playing was getting slower, until finally the guitar just sort of petered out in the middle of a song and I nodded off and fell into my microphone stand. I woke up immediately, caught the stand before it fell, and started another song.

Oddly, being a burnt-out lounge musician seemed to be attracting more women followers on board. Whether they were thirsty for my blood or just had a motherly, nursing instinct kick in, I'm not sure. I was just trying to survive. But I'd start to get notes on cocktail napkins that said things like, "Dear hot lounge singer, we love the way you strum the guitar. Come up to room 307 and strum us. XXOO."

It wasn't until the final two weeks, when someone almost put a hole through Meal-ticket by dropping a nickel from nine stories up, that I really lost my shit. 'Fuck it. I don't care if I get fired,' I decided. I'd start to do four-hour sets of only guitar, never singing or speaking a word, just playing the same riffs over and over. Other times I'd pop an extra pill and sing as hard as I could just to see what I could handle, and what death metal folk would sound like. There would be a sheer tearing pain rippling through my chest as I screamed out 'House of the Rising Sun.' At any moment I half-expected my vocal cords to snap and go flying out of my mouth like rubber bands. This was the stupidest way I could have handled my situation, and I'm lucky I didn't permanently ruin my voice, but I wanted off the boat.

I met some attractive college soccer players and invited one back to my cabin in the crew area. We walked past security officers and stepped into the glass elevator where we made out for a ten-floor descent, her tongue darting in and out of my mouth like a nervous sparrow. Then we walked past more security officers, and through the "Crew Only" door that led to the hall outside my cabin. The officers saw what I was doing. They could have had me fired. I wasn't trying to be sneaky.

I was ready for J.D. to give me the pink slip at any time. Finally one day he came up to me and said, "You're free to leave when we get to New York today. You've finished your first Festival contract."

I sighed with relief. The war was over.

"By the way," J.D. said. "You should consider going to Austin, Texas. Your music fits the catalogue, and I think you'd like it."

"Thanks, boss," I said.

I was wrecked, but I had made it. I had more money leaving that job than I had ever had before in my life. I enjoyed it for a week or two and then put most of it towards college debts. I had also left the cruise ship with that nice microphone that the audio technician loaned me my first night. I considered it a retirement gift to myself.

Back in Wisconsin, hugging my van, I promised never to leave it again. Then I climbed into the front seat, and had a long summer's nap.

DRIVING IN CIRCLES

I bummed around Wisconsin for a month or two and worked on resting up. I didn't sing a note the entire time, and very rarely pulled Meal-ticket out of its case. I did drop in on my parents to say hello and enjoy some of the home cooked meals I was raised on. I crashed at my friends' houses, but kept my visits a little more low-key than the last drunken joy ride I took around the state.

I was staying at my friend Rod's house when I really started reassessing my situation. I inspected the van and all my worldly possessions crammed inside of it. Then I started pulling all my clothes, books, broken kazoos and everything else I'd accumulated out and tossed each item into one of three piles in Rod's yard: the Goodwill store pile, the pile of things to keep, and the burn pile.

Once I had all my junk sorted, I took a measuring tape and measured the open space in the back of the van. I drove to a nearby army surplus store, leaving everything out in Rod's lawn. At the surplus store there was an army cot that was the perfect size. I bought it, popped it open, and set it up in the back of the van. Then I drove back to my worldly heaps.

I started to reload my pans, tools and instruments from the pile of things to keep back into the minivan. The cot was perfect. The bigger things fit into the space around it, and the smaller items fit underneath it. No more being crunched and uncomfortable trying to sleep across the front seats. Nor would I ever need to check into a motel or campground again.

I would be traveling in style from then on.

Once I had the van the way I wanted, I walked past the last two piles and into Rod's house. I tossed him the van keys.

"What's this about?" he asked looking at the keys.

"I got a new addition to the van; I want to try it out. You drive."

"What's with all the shit in my yard?" he asked as we walked out his door.

"You can have anything in the pile on the left. The rest of that pile is going to Goodwill."

"What about the pile on the right?"

"Let's have a bonfire tonight."

"Oh... burning your paper trail?"

"Something like that."

He got into the driver's seat and I opened the sliding back door and hopped onto the cot.

"Nice cot," he said. "Is that the fancy new van addition?"

"Sure is."

He started the van. "Where should we go?"

"I don't know, Rod. You're the driver. Maybe the liquor store to get whiskey for the bonfire tonight?"

"Will do."

"Luxury!" I yelled as the van started moving down the street. "You know, people pay big bucks to ride like this in ambulances. I get it anytime I want now for free."

Rod laughed and said, "You know, you could start a traveling psychology business in here. Drive right up to the patients' doors, have them come into your office-van and lie down on the cot. You could hold sessions as you do your errands."

He took a hard turn and I held on tight to the creaky cot. "Brilliant," I said. "With this cot, the possibilities are endless."

"Tell me what's been on your mind of late?" Rod asked in a sloppy accent that fell somewhere between German and British.

"Funny you should ask, Doctor Jekyll. There's been a lot on my mind."

"Go on," he said stroking his chin.

"Well I've been in what you might call an existential funk. I don't really know what to do with myself. I want to keep traveling and hobo-ing, but I'm also on vocal rest. I almost ruined myself on that cruise gig. I could still travel, but I wouldn't be able to sing any money in."

"Ya. Zat ist a problem."

"Yes, so I started thinking that maybe I'd go to a new town and just stay in one place until I recover."

"Why not stay here?"

"I've lived here. It's familiar. I want something new and unknown."

"You won't ever be satisfied with that attitude. The moment you've lived somewhere for a while it will become old and you'll want to go somewhere else. You'll never be happy anywhere for long."

"By new and unknown, I just meant different. Things are nice here. There's nothing wrong with this place. It's a great place to settle down. I just want something different for now."

"Where are you thinking?"

"I opened the atlas the other day and happened to land on L.A., but looking at all the yellow urban sprawl of the greater Los Angeles area, I felt kind of intimidated. I don't think I'm ready for Hollywood."

"Or maybe Hollywood isn't ready for you."

"Thank you Doctor Kevorkian. You are too kind. The next page I flipped to was Eastern Texas, and Austin stuck out to me."

"Austin is the live music capitol of the world they say."

"I've heard that the economy is pretty good there, and my cruise ship boss recommended I check it out. Also there was this girl I met who was hula-hooping on a mountain top in Missoula. She said all her friends were moving to Austin."

"So you're going to move there to hang out with her friends?"

"No. Well, maybe. I don't know. It just seems like the signs are all pointing to Austin."

Rod came to an abrupt stop and my head hit the front passenger seat. "We're at the liquor store," he said cutting the engine. "That will be ten dollars, or a bottle of whiskey."

"I'm going to buy us a bottle of whiskey," I said opening the side door and sliding off the cot to the pavement. "I'm going to get us some whiskey and soak my vocal cords in it like a new harmonica."

"I got dibs on the cot for the ride back," Rod said.

"Deal."

I decided to take the Great River Road for the long ride south. The road starts at the swampy headwaters of the Mississippi River in northern Minnesota, and follows the muddy all the way down to the Gulf of Mexico. I think I would have done well in the small river towns along the way had I been up to performing.

When I used my guitar as a way to break the ice and meet people, most of my music hobo-trips were a tour of America's cultural geography. With a guitar it's easy to get to know the folks that frequent the bars and diners in any region. You learn the general overall attitude that people hold towards things. If I hit the right song at the right time, I often found myself 'best friends' with a stranger for that night, for better or worse.

Since I wasn't playing music on this drive, it was to be a whole different kind of trip. This one was turning into a physical geography drive of sorts. Which wasn't bad; there's plenty to see in every part of the country. But when you're traveling alone and don't really get to know the people, the whole journey can leave you with a kind of empty feeling. And maybe that's what I was searching for in a base-camp as I skipped from city to city: not so much the place, but the people that I met in that place.

I was mulling this over when I noticed the Great River Road getting a little less than great as it turned to gravel and led me through a corn field. I was convinced that someone had taken and moved the road signs to a poor farmer's drive-way as a prank. I sensed I was going to end up at a dead end by a red barn. Thankfully though, after about five miles the Great (gravel portion of the) River Road had gone all the way through the massive corn field and I was back on a highway.

I stayed at a parking lot in northern Missouri or southern Iowa that night, getting my first good night's rest on the modernized technology of the van cot.

The next day, I put on my tourist hat in the town of Hannibal. This was Samuel Clemens' hometown, or as the welcome sign put it: "America's Hometown." It's true that it was the basis for the setting of Tom Sawyer and some of Huck Finn, so in a way most Americans are familiar with the town. The Old Town section of Hannibal did have that Mark Twain Americana feel to it. Whether or not it was an atmosphere that was manufactured for the sake of tourism, I couldn't tell. Every building was named after a character or place in a Twain book, and the museum there was filled with Norman Rockwell paintings. I paid my homage to Huck, Tom, and Samuel at a statue of his two most famous characters looking out over the river and continued.

Missouri is a long state. Misery is a long state ... especially at night. At some point I lost the scent of the Great River Road and realized I was quite a ways west of the river. Austin was west of the river anyway, so I went with it.

In Oklahoma, I drove an hour out of my way to see Okemah, Woody Guthrie's hometown. Once an oil boomtown, Okemah was now a single main street with a few struggling businesses frequented mostly by tumbleweeds. Every year they had a festival in honor of Woody, but other than that there isn't much of a reason to stop there. I sought out and found the slab of concrete that Woody had signed his name into when the sidewalk was new and he was a child. I traced the letters with my finger.

The drive had transcended a physical geography trip and was turning into a history lesson-style pilgrimage.

A little north of Dallas, the van engine started to make funny noises. I wasn't laughing. I brought it to a mechanic with my stomach in knots. A thousand worries raced through my head. 'What do I do if the van is wrecked? I can't afford a new car. Will I have to move into this Dallas suburb? Could I actually make it as a real hobo instead of a tire tramp?'

"Where you from?" the mechanic asked me.

"Wisconsin. Like the plates say," I said.

"Ah Wisconsin. I been there. They got some nice towns. They got some nice prisons too. I did time in Waupun."

"Oh. Good," I said and handed him the van keys.

While he was fixing the van, I walked across the street to a Mexican restaurant with Meal-ticket to see how rusty my voice was and also if I could raise some money for the repairs. I taped a sign to the inside of my guitar case lid saying: "Wisconsin musician en route to Austin. Vehicle currently broke down and in the shop across the street. Tips appreciated."

I gave my sales pitch to the manager, and was met with a very enthusiastic yes. It was my first time playing a Mexican restaurant, but it would not be my last. I learned in the years to come that Mexican restaurants were more likely to allow a musician to play than other places. I don't know if this is a cultural thing or what, but I do know that on that day there weren't many customers and I still raised eighty dollars.

It cost $200 to get the serpentine belt wheel bearing replaced. It was a small price to pay to have the van back in operation, plowing down the highway into the heart of Texas like a stake into a vampire.

My brother-in-law, Tony, had given me the number for a campground near Austin. "They're friends of my family," he said. "They're your kind of people. Just call them up and drop my name."

The campground was carved out of a cedar tree forest and dotted with snarls of mesquite. It was designed specifically for RVs and horse rigs. Each site had about two or three horse pens near it, and was equipped with electricity and water. There was also a bungalow which looked like a small, human-sized doll house, plus a couple of pit toilet outhouses, and two outdoor showers.

"Now normally we don't allow non-horse people to camp here," Helen, a tie-dye-clad woman with brownish-gray, curly hair told me. "But as you're a friend of the family, and the place is empty at the moment, you can stay. You can stay at least until horse people need your site."

"Understood, and thank you," I said and began setting the old tent up in an out-of-the-way spot by the privy. I was looking forward to an overdue shower under the Texas moon.

The next morning I went into town and began an apartment search. I went to a free realtor's service that I had seen advertised in the local paper, and the realtor took me on a tour of a few properties. The first seemed to already be inhabited by a colony of cockroaches. Several bug bodies lay scattered through the kitchen and bathroom like confetti at a New Year's party in a dumpster. The other apartment was way out of my price range. Both came with six-month contracts, which I had learned is an awfully long time.

I checked out an open mic after the fruitless apartment search. The place was filled with my artistic kin: dirty, broke musicians.

I felt my vocal cords were up to the task, so I did a few originals. The crowd was very attentive. It was a little unnerving to play for a group of people that weren't noisy and drunken as I had become used to.

Afterwards a skinny musician with a wispy mustache and a vintage golf hat who had played a few slots before me walked over and said, "Welcome to Austin. You sounded good up there. I'm Blake."

"Nice to meet you, Blake. You're not so bad yourself," I said and nodded at him. "I'm D.B."

"Yeah man," Blake told me later over a beer, "everyone in this town and their pet plays guitar and writes songs. Everywhere you go here is like a jam session. It truly is the live music capitol of the world."

"My kind of place," I said.

"Another thing you'll notice about Austin is that hardly anyone who lives here is from here. And the folks that have lived here for a while romanticize a smaller, older Austin. The general vibe with the Austin veterans is that this place was a lot cooler before you and everyone else moved in, and you are partially to blame for this un-coolness."

"Oh. That's nice. A real welcoming bunch."

"Ha. Not all the old Austin elite are like that, but many are. For all us newly-moved-in kids though, it's like an exciting camping trip of sorts. We're all in this together, you know."

"How long have you been here, Blake?"

"About six months. And yes, it was a cooler place before you got here. And yes, I do blame you. You in particular." He smiled while taking a drink.

I went back to camp in the dark and had a little campfire. I was practicing some tricks I had picked up at the open mic, when Helen appeared in the light of the fire on a classic-looking bicycle.

"A musician," she said. "Imagine that."

I couldn't tell if she was being sarcastic or not.

"My husband Bud and I have just started playing guitar. You sing too?"

"Yup."

"Let's hear one."

I played Helen a song I had written called 'Every Orchard' about working the blueberry fields in Maine.

"Very nice!" she said.

I thanked her and gave her a CD.

"Come on by the house tomorrow evening and I'll feed you dinner and we'll play some music."

"Okay."

"You know where the house is?"

"Is it the one across the big horse pasture there?"

"Yessir. See you tomorrow."

I woke up the next morning to the sound of pounding. Peeking out of my tent, I saw a man wearing overalls with a shaggy, gray beard and long, salt-and-pepper hair pulled back into a ponytail. He was straightening out the bar of a horse pen with a hammer. When he left, I got up and readied myself for town.

It was another day spent apartment searching. I found one through Craigslist that was within my price range and had a three-month lease. The place was a nursing home, turned music co-op, turned apartment building. Because of its nursing home origins, it had tile floors and bed-size-wide doors. It had a very institutional feel. Every room shared a bathroom with a neighboring room, and there was one kitchen for the whole place shared by everyone. I filled out the paperwork and would be able to move in a few days after.

When I got back to camp I saw that a horse rig had moved into a nearby campsite and a horse was occupying the pen that the man had been working on that morning. Around dinner time I walked through the pasture with Meal-ticket to Helen's home and knocked on the door. She opened it and said, "Perfect timing, come on in for grub."

On the kitchen table were a big pot of a chili-like substance, a pot of rice, and a giant bowl of a spinach-based salad.

"Bud! Time to eat!" Helen shouted through a hall off of the kitchen. "Well dig in," she said to me.

I grabbed a little metal bowl and threw some spinach salad into it and topped it off with balsamic vinegar and olive oil.

Bud came in and sat across from me at the table. He was the fellow who had been hammering in the morning.

Helen sat down between us and introduced us officially.

"I met Bud when I was selling T-shirts on the drag downtown," Helen said.

"She invited me out here to ride horses with her in the park," Bud chimed in. "She rides fast."

"Yeah, I used to invite a lot of guys riding, but I think it was a little more than most could handle," Helen said with a smile. "Bud was the only one who came back to ride again."

"It took some guts, I'm not gonna lie," Bud said smiling

and looking at Helen.

"So is that the horse riding park right up the road?" I asked.

"Yessir," Helen said. "Best horse park in Texas. And I'm their best customer."

"They were thinking about shutting the park down for a while," Bud added. "Not enough people were using it because there was no place to stay with their horses. It wasn't worth it to come here from Dallas or Houston if you had to drive back at the end of the day. Helen came up with the idea of the camp and basically saved the park."

I started digging into the chili and rice.

"So you know Marjorie?" Helen asked.

Marjorie was my brother-in-law's mother. I had met her a few times, and played her some music. "Yeah, she's Tony's mom. Nice lady," I said.

"Well Marjorie is the whole reason I moved down here. I'm from Wisconsin too. She called me up one day when she was living here and said, 'Helen, come down to Austin. The people are friendly, the rent is cheap, and the good times are everywhere.' So I got my suitcase and hitched down here with seventy-five dollars in my pocket."

"That must have been quite a trip," I said.

"It was. When I first got here I wanted to take up harmonica and join a band. I was trying to find Willie Nelson's harmonica player, Mickey Raphael. I was going to take lessons from him. But I gave up music once I realized how much drinking it was going to involve. I couldn't keep up. So I learned how to airbrush T-shirts and how to make tile art. I sold my wares at the drag downtown and eventually took up the renaissance fair circuit. I'm done with all that now. Got the campground."

I was just about stuffed by that point. I was looking at my empty bowl and trying to decide if it would be impolite to take a third helping.

"Save room," said Bud. "There's peach cobbler and whipped cream for dessert."

I quickly put my hand up to my chin to catch my dropping jaw.

"When we built the campground," Bud explained, "we

thought the campers would naturally be cowboy musicians in the style of Gene Autry and Tex Ritter. We were expecting to hear a lot of music, but hardly anyone ever brought an instrument here. It's a big part of the whole horse-camp experience and it was missing. We decided if we wanted to have music, we'd have to bring it to camp ourselves."

Helen got up, took the warm peach cobbler out of the oven and set it on the table. "We listened to your CD," she said. "I was very impressed with it. Let's play some music after dessert."

My mouth was full so I just nodded in agreement.

We were tuning guitars in the living room when Bud asked, "How are you liking Austin so far?"

"It's fun so far. Rent is kind of expensive, but I found a place. I'll be moving into it in a couple of days."

"Rent didn't used to be so high in town," Bud said. "Austin has become a strange music boomtown of sorts. It's the last liberal haven in a red state."

"What are you going to do for work?" Helen asked.

"Not sure yet. I want to work the music scene, but my voice is still kind of in recovery mode from the cruise ship gig. I think I might just look for a part-time job in the meantime."

We jammed for about an hour, Bud and I on guitars, and Helen singing. Helen had an honest cowgirl's voice. She sounded like a female version of Willie Nelson. They played a lot of traditional cowboy and ranch songs like 'Red River Valley' and 'Back in the Saddle': perfect songs for singing around the fire at a horse camp.

I could tell they were beginners, but they had a good, natural feel. I showed them a few chords and strumming tricks and said goodnight.

The new apartment in town still smelled like old people, and late at night I sometimes thought I heard hospital beds being wheeled down the hall. I often heard the neighbor I shared a bathroom with vomiting early in the morning. I'm pretty sure he was an alcoholic. The place was also infested with dust bunnies. I couldn't get rid of them and eventually had to learn to peacefully coexist with them.

I worked the coffee shop open mic circuit in town, seeing a handful of the same faces at each one. Blake talked me into going to an open blues jam at a biker bar one night. "You gotta hear these blues players. They're from the old school of blues ... Chicago style. They let you go up and play with them. It'd be like we had our own band."

So I drove us to the Roadhouse Bar about thirty minutes south of Austin. We walked into the dim bar and our eyes adjusted to the filthy surroundings dimly illuminated by neon lights. There were several tables of bikers, leather-clad, with the patches, emblems, and colors of their particular gangs. They seemed like pirates to me with their bandannas and the few days' growth of whiskers on their faces, toasting each other with pints that were frothing over and screaming with the incredible blues band that was playing. Blake and I looked like tidy hipster preps compared to them. There was one other guy who was clearly not a biker, but had come from Austin to play music. He signed up to play when we did. But after fidgeting nervously at the bar and watching the house band jam for a while, he got up, quickly walked out the front door with his guitar, and we never saw him again. They called me up to play, and as Blake is a guitarist of somewhat virtuosic ability, I asked that he come up and play lead with me.

With the house bass player and drummer thumping the groove and Blake shrieking a solo or two, we wandered through a few blues standards that I knew: 'How Long Blues,' and 'Hoochie Coochie Man.' The bikers were respectful and dismissive to us for the most part. We probably looked like a couple of amateurs who got their kicks by being around a dangerous, seedy crowd. The last song I chose to play was the Doors song, 'Roadhouse Blues.' It seemed appropriate because we were at the Roadhouse Bar. While we were playing, a biker got up with his girl and they started dancing and grinding on each other right in front of us. I took this as a good sign. The biker looked like a football player. His head was shaved clean. He had no shirt, but was wearing a leather vest and had leather pants with a studded belt. His lady was also donned in leather over a tank top. She had blonde hair cut just below her ears, and looked like she could have been a model on an 80s hairband record cover when she was younger, but lifestyle and years were catching up to her.

After 'Roadhouse Blues' Blake and I thanked the audience and band and returned to the bar for a victory beer. I took a stool next to Blake and had just gotten my first sip of beer when the blonde dancer came over to us and said, "Ohhh, you guys were so cute up there. Group hug!" She leaned in to hug me and Blake on our respective stools, and over her shoulder I could see her muscle-bound, bald dancing partner giving us the stink eye with his arms crossed.

She squeezed us in a hug, and I reached my arm out to the biker behind her trying to bring him in it or at least make him lighten up, and said to him, "Group hug?"

The blonde lady walked away and the biker walked over. He looked at me very intensely and said, "I just wanted to say thanks for playing Roadhouse Blues."

"No problem?"

Then he started shouting. "I was going to play that fucking song tonight and now I can't!" He grabbed both sides of my head above my ears and started squeezing my head like a pimple. "What am I supposed to play now, you little son of a bitch? You come down here from Austin and think you kids are such hot shit." He was screaming as loudly as possible, directly into my left ear. I thought it was going to start bleeding. I mumbled something to the effect of, "I'm sorry. I swear I won't play it next week, 'Roadhouse Blues' is all yours from now on."

After squeezing and shaking my head for a bit while Blake sat on the stool next to me confused as hell, the biker started laughing and dropped his hands. "I'm just fucking with you. My name is Chug." He offered his hand for a handshake, and as I put my hand out to his, he pulled a knife from his pants with his other hand, pointed it closely at me for a good, long ten seconds, and then flipped it over and tried to give it to Blake.

"Here," Chug said to Blake. "Stab him in the heart."

I wish I would have remembered that I had a Swiss army knife in my pocket at that point, because I would have pulled it out and said the same thing to Blake but with Chug as the victim, and Blake would have been sitting there with two knives in his hands not sure what to do.

Then Chug started laughing again, sheathed his knife and walked away. Blake and I scrammed. The next day I had a gig booked through a friend to play at a knife-throwing convention. I was very anxious about it, but luckily Chug was not in attendance.

I tried to figure out the bar music scene in Austin by walking up and down the infamous Sixth Street, which was vibrant with all its starry-eyed drunks in short skirts and beggars with guitars at every corner. I asked the barkeep at every venue I went past how I should go about booking a show. It turned out there were a handful of booking agents in town that the majority of the bars worked through. In order to get a gig at these venues, you had to sort of court the booking agents.

The smaller cafes were a different matter: no agent to go through, just shoot an e-mail or go talk to the manager and you had a gig. I started booking shows with Blake. I was easing my vocal cords back into performance mode.

"I'm glad to be playing, but I wish some of these gigs paid," I told him before one of our shows.

"Why would they pay us? You see the handful of people in the audience right now? Each one of them is a musician. They're not necessarily watching us; they might just be waiting their turn. Why pay any of us when there are thousands of musicians outside the door who would love to play a show here and would do it for free. The place is saturated with musicians."

"Hmmm. Maybe we should unionize?" I suggested.

"Ha. Austin does give free health care if you can prove that you're a resident and play at least three shows a year.

But the truth of the matter is that you don't come to Austin to make money playing music. You can make money off the musicians, by opening a music store or venue, making album art or music videos, or becoming a booking agent, or teaching guitar lessons, but musicians typically don't make money here. Austin is more like a ridiculously fun, hard-knock music school for us musicians. "

"Oh," I said.

"Class dismissed," he finished.

So with my job search not going anywhere and the odds of scraping by with music seemingly slim, my feet started doing their happy little 'Let's get out of Dodge' dance. But I was locked in a three-month contract to my apartment. I decided to just try and enjoy myself, hopefully recover, and learn from this municipal music class.

One night Helen called my cell phone. "What are you doing tomorrow night?"

"Nothing as of yet."

"Come on out to camp for dinner and a jam."

"Will do."

The following night, after a feast and a solid rehearsal, Bud said, "Why don't we make this a once-a-week thing. You come out and jam with us, and we'll feed you."

"Count me in," I said.

I courted one of the smaller booking agents with flattery and free CDs and eventually landed a regular weekly gig at the Galapagos Bar on Sixth Street. 'Hitting the big time now,' I thought to myself. I could feel the strength returning to my vocal cords with each performance.

The Sixth Street gig was like the cruise ship gig in certain ways. The majority of people that came in were tourists who had heard of the magical, musical Sixth Street in the middle of Austin. Except that this audience was also peppered with a few local college students and musicians. Pay was ten percent of the drinks that were sold in the hour I was playing. Sometimes I'd get fifty dollars with a bunch of tips on top. Other times I'd get ten dollars and no tips at all.

It can be extremely frustrating as an artist in a place like this. I could see Blake and others go through these cycles of being in love with the town, then hopelessly depressed and angry at it: the Austin doldrums.

On those off nights at the bar, those nights when I played to an audience of empty barstools and it seemed like nothing I did would ever be good enough, I'd fall into the Austin doldrums too. I'd sit at the bar after my set watching the next act, and drink down every last dollar I had just earned. Then I'd stumble back to the nursing home, down dark alleys, scattering my CDs on the ground like flower petals that no one would ever smell.

The jam sessions continued once a week at Helen and Bud's. We even began performing for the campers and their horses once in a while. They were warm little affairs around campfires. We'd play traditional cowboy music, as sparks flew from the fire and mingled with shooting stars in the sky. It was a great contrast to playing in town. I was even able to sell the guests some of my CDs, and on top of that, Helen insisted on paying me. I was making more money at camp than in town.

After a jam one evening, Bud said to me, "You know, there's a songwriting symposium coming to town in a month. You write good songs. You should seriously consider going and shopping them to the Nashville publishers that run the thing."

"Really? Does it cost anything?"

"I think it's something like $200," Bud said.

I wondered if it was just another scheme to make money off the musicians.

"I can't afford it," I said.

"What? No luck with work in town?" Helen asked.

"Not exactly, no."

"Well we got plenty of work you could do here," Helen said.

"I don't know."

"How does fifteen dollars an hour sound?"

"I'm in," I said without thinking. "What kind of work are we talking about?"

"You ever scooped horse manure before?" Bud asked with a grin.

I drove out to the campground every afternoon and worked until dark. They'd feed me dinner and we'd often play music afterwards. Work consisted of mucking horse stalls and pens, mowing the campground, fence and trail maintenance, shredding the pasture on a tractor, and herding hens.

They had a handful of chickens that roamed the grounds freely. Every night I'd help round up the hens and get them safely into a plywood and welded-wire hen house. Since they weren't laying eggs, we'd usually leave the roosters out at night to fend for themselves. They'd peck a hole in your hand if you tried to pick them up anyway. If they were bigger, I think they would have slaughtered all of us. I remember walking through the barn one day with the feeling that I was being followed. I turned around and a rooster was standing five steps behind me, pecking at the ground and acting generally innocent. I walked out of the barn and looked over my shoulder to see the rooster racing after me.

When I turned all the way around though, it stopped a couple steps short of me and pretended it wasn't in pursuit. I slowly backed away from it and it ran after me again. The rooster had its red feathers puffed out in attack mode. It was either me or the rooster so when it made a lunge at my ankles, I gave it a firm boot to its chest. Feathers flew in all directions and it crowed at me, but it didn't follow me again.

I had always been kind of nervous around horses. They are giant creatures and could cause a lot of damage if they're in a bad disposition. Helen taught me how to be comfortable around the horses but to always respect them and their space. She taught me the feeding schedules of the goofy Tennessee Walking Horse and the incredibly friendly red Quarter Horse she and Bud owned.

It didn't take long for me to raise the $200 that I needed for the symposium, but Helen and Bud insisted that I keep coming to work and play music. So I did.

The big day of the symposium came, and I put on my finest T-shirt and polished up Meal-ticket. I thought I might get my 'big break' that day.

In a hotel conference room, I played three original songs for three Nashville publishers. "These are good songs," one of them said, "but I don't know who we could shop them to. They seem to be very much your own. Maybe try writing one with a particular pop star in mind."

Another publisher said, "We always tell people to learn the rules of songwriting and then forget them. With you, I would recommend going back to learn the rules of songwriting again."

The last publisher said, "The words you use are too big. No one will know what 'Pirouettes' or 'Effigy' means. You have to kind of imagine that you're playing for a bunch of rich five year olds. That's basically what the people are."

I couldn't believe that last publisher. If you keep dumbing down art/products, the culture/consumers will remain dumb, maybe even regress. We'd have a country filled with idiots. Why not push people to be smarter? Is being smart a bad thing?

Maybe we are in a dark age of some sort. Stupidity isn't only being encouraged, it's being cultivated. It's easier to make money and control people when they are dumber than you.

After I thought about it for a while, I started to feel like the suggestion that my lyrics were 'too smart' for pop culture was a compliment. Yet I was still disappointed deep down. My value system was embedded with pop culture, prompting me to crave acceptance and money. I had hoped that at least one publisher would take an interest in my work and shop it somewhere. I could have used the validation and encouragement. I could have used the possible money. It would have somehow helped me feel that my whole life's work had not been in vain.

I took a breath, a step back, and said to myself, 'Screw it. I don't need approval or validation from some pop culture-pushing publisher jerks. The fact that I'm living off my songs and music is validation enough. The only standards that I really need to live up to are my own. I'm not going to lower them and change the way I write for monetary ends. And this life has never been in vain, if only because I've loved every perfect and terrible minute of it. It hasn't been in vain because I've spread this love to others as much as I could in my travels and with my music.'

Month three ended at the Austin nursing home. I thanked Helen and Bud and hit the road. My vocal cords felt strong and I was ready for the adventure to continue. I'd forgotten how much the van liked to move. Oh, how it could ramble. I would just kick my seat back and let the van take me wherever it wanted to go.

It made a stop at the Bonnie and Clyde Massacre Museum in Louisiana. This was the last building the notorious bank robbers had entered alive before being riddled with hundreds of bullets a few miles later.

The man running it was a seventy-year-old, chain-smoking cancer survivor, a free mason, an ex-FBI agent, and the son of one of the men who massacred Bonnie and Clyde. After checking out the museum, I couldn't help myself. I pulled out Meal-ticket and played the museum clerk a bank-robbing song I had written while he smoked another cigarette on the sidewalk out front. Other museum tourists stopped to listen too. After I finished, he croaked, "Yahp. That's a Clyde song." Then he walked back in the museum as I sold a few CDs to the tourists.

A little further down the line, I passed a shotgun shack bar outside of Jackson, Mississippi. It looked just like a bar I had luck playing in Montana once. I entered and stopped in my tracks immediately. I was not in Montana. The jukebox was blaring disco music, and half of the twenty-odd people there were dressed like pimps from the seventies. There I was, the only white person walking into a bar, in the land where the blues began, with an acoustic guitar in my hands. Who did I think I was fooling?

Everyone stopped what they were doing to stare me down. I almost turned around and continued driving, but I figured I'd come this far so I might as well ask.

I went to the bartender and gave a shaky pitch. She almost grudgingly said, "Okay. But only after the jukebox plays out."

So I took a seat at the bar and nervously sipped some water as I waited. The man on the stool next to me looked over and said, "So you play for tips, huh?"

"Yes."

"Here's a tip. Go on back home," then he turned away from me.

After a few more jukebox songs, a different bartender came over to me and said, "Well, I think you'll be on after this song. The stage is over there in the corner." I looked in the direction he was pointing and saw a small stage with a pole. "And listen, man," he went on, "I don't know what's going to happen next, but here's a few bucks just for having the courage to come in here and ask to play." He held three dollars out towards me.

"No, no," I waved the money away. "Wait until you've heard me sing."

I played a set of mostly blues and R&B songs, winning the approval of almost everyone there. I earned forty dollars in about half an hour, but the real payout from that stop was the adrenalin rush that came when I got up on stage to play. Everything else in the world melted away. It was just me with my guitar in that moment, and there was nothing else. It felt like the first time I had played a concert all over again, and I remembered why I originally started doing this.

I flipped through the atlas randomly as I lay on my cot that night. As long as I was in Mississippi, I thought I might as well go to the blues museum in Clarksdale; maybe even find Robert Johnson's crossroads. Then what? I had heard that there were goat farms looking for help in North Carolina. I heard there was big money out in the oil boomtowns of North Dakota.

'Yes,' I decided. 'I'll do that. All of that. As long as I got Meal-ticket, I can find a supper somewhere, and as long as I got supper, I'm going to keep on running.'

Joy Ride into the Night

I'm the captain of this here mini-van,
and I'm driving it across this mass of land.
From sea to shining sea, and everywhere between.
I'm on a joy ride into the night.
My guitar's got a name and it's Meal-Ticket.
And every chance I get I'm going to pick it.
I've played every street from Chicago to New Orleans,
I'm on a joy ride into the night.
Once I tried to stay and settle down.
I got a home in a little lonesome town,
but I woke up one day and I threw it all away,
I'm on a joy ride into the night.
I'm the captain of this here mini-van,
and I'm driving it across this massive land.
From sea to shining sea, and everywhere between.
I'm on a joy ride into the night.

-D.B. Rouse

"Joy Ride into the Night" is available on the book soundtrack **Meal-Ticket**, at your nearest iTunes or Amazon.com store.

THE BIG BENDER

Actual text from a road journal excavated from the
van by Rod Kouba, Blake Langlinais, and D.B. Rouse

5/29/2010
3:49 AM

What is Texas?

This one started about 2 hours ago at Dallas/Fort Worth Intl Airport. We're heading SW to a Folk Festival to undoubtedly see some un-Texas thing. Ben turned at a sign for a historical marker and it turned into us going the wrong way down a one way. No lessons learned.

-The plan as of now is to drive through the day and end up at Big Bend 3:55, make it happen.

7:36 AM

When in roam, roam. When in Texas, indulge.

Rouse is passed out from a night of cigarettes, beer, coffee, and chain driving. Or isn't binge driving more appropriate? Either way, I slept through miles of conversation, gallons of smoke (tobacco), and hours of <drinking(crossed out)> pit-stops. We are going to get to Kerrville at about 8:30 am, so maybe there will be time for adventure and fun. Hopefully Rouse will come around so he can enjoy the hippy fest, which is not looking likely.

We played at a cafe for tips yesterday, which was great, made $17 in 45 minutes, so we could cover some of the costs. If all goes well, we make it to Big Bend, and if it goes better than we expected, we make it back in good shape.

11:33 AM

625 miles since 5 pm yesterday.

It feels like it should be later in the day.

Blake is driving now- shakily- He is not used to the Blood Drop Van we call home.

Rod, after having some sort of stomach bug, is passed out asleep again in back. Seems to be feeling better since a good breakfast of Kolaches.

I should be sleeping. I nodded off while driving only moments ago. But I can't. Maybe it's because I took a 5 hour energy drink with my 10:30 AM beer. Maybe it's because I'm worried about Blake's driving skills.

Had driven us into the sunrise. The landscape revealed itself in the foggy morning moonlight- Rolling green/brown hills w/ snarls of mesquite sticking every which way.

I pulled over and played Rod some of my new songs at sunrise (all jittery like). He seemed relatively un-impressed or very tired.

Blake took over to Kerrville. We found the festival grounds. $40/ person/ night.

Said 'Fuck it.' and drove away up a large hill.

Desolate wonderful landscape. Vultures picking the eyes out of a deer on the roadside.

Crop dusting plane right beside us. Dusting the crop, and leaving the van misted in pesticide.

Not far from Bandera- saw 2 horse riders riding in the middle of the road (opposite), flagging us over to the side. We pulled over and saw that a cop car with lights flashing was following them. I became quickly paranoid that it was an alcohol check point of some sort... and seeing as I was already half drunk on that fine and sunny morning, and that the car seats were balanced on stacks of empty Lone Star Beer... Luckily it was a parade. A Texas parade if ever there was one. 100 or so horses, bunch of wagons... and here we are parading without a license. We waited ten or fifteen minutes for them to pass, chatted a little bit with one of the flagmen on horse back... he made mention of some dude and his horse being hit by a car the other day.

After they passed, we drove on towards Bandera. Near the outskirts of town we saw a lively rodeo ring and a campground with a bunch of giant BBQ grills and tents. We stopped to investigate.

Found out by chatting with a BBQ chef that we were walking in the midst of a BBQ tourney. We got the scoop, and then asked for a scoop of BBQ. No such luck. Rodeo was supposed to start at 8pm. That would leave a lot of down time between the morning and then.

Still, I felt like we should find a cheap motel and stay for it. This would have been a true 'texperience'. but no cheap motel in sight. And the guys have big bend eyes. So we push on.

'Road Trip'- Endurance Contest.

Starting to feel like a Vegas style death march. But it's far too early to call it a 'death' march. It's a march all right, but to what? I know not.

The car already smells a bit of funk, as I sit in the seat where ----- wet and vomited on herself last week. A funk that would match our mood, if not for Blake's infectious good spirit. I guess I can't say Rod is in a funk as he is very busy sleeping.

Maybe a sweet sweet Dublin Dr. Pepper from the toothless Mississippian is in order.

Saturday Evening, Alpine TX, Motel Bien Venidos

So we pushed it, made it about 80 miles north of the park. We tried to stay east of here in Marathon, but true to its name, the motel lady sold us on going to Alpine and continuing the marathon, the death march... or more accurately, the trail of beers. How did we get from there to Marathon? Short answer TX ST HWY 90.

MANY BAD TEQUILAS

"I lie to people to make me the gas money. That makes me a liar."

"It's not about anything, man."

Here is what is tough. Double regret scenarios. Should we have paid $40 to go to the hippy folk festival? Only God knows. I can imagine many scenarios that could have taken place in there to make it worth it. And the Texas BBQ and rodeo competition we skipped? That almost definitely seems like a mistake to skip even now. But we had to move on. Why that is, you could write a book about. So much can happen either way. It is, I suppose, incorrect to think we 'did anything wrong' here. It's supposed to be all random anyway. Shit. Point is, we made it to Big Bend.

Those other things would have been awesome no doubt, but this is right because it is the way we went. It's the whole point of the thing. There should be no regret for the paths that should have, could have been taken. It's an inspection of double negative thinking. Go on and do.

That said. The 1%ers:

Like we talked about earlier, the Marathon lady talked us into going on to the next town. Alpine. We couldn't get a room in Marathon, and considering the fatigue involved in driving there from Dallas, we were effectively marooned now, in this city. And here we have a good objective example of the appeal of a chaotic entity from the outside, starkly compared to the reality of being stuck in the situation. The 1%ers.

I was driving, it was earlier on 90, no where to say the least. No other cars, no need to pay attention. What seemed out of no where, the van was being pursued by a horde of cycles. It was a real gang. They certainly looked the part. They had the vests festooned with the club logo. The Bandidos. And what the hell did we know? For the sake of a good story, we afforded them all the attributes of an outlaw motorcycle club.

So I pull over and let them pass; 25 or so. Half of them waved a biker code kind of wave. Code of respect kind of thing.

New pen, new day. That last thing written in a bad drunken haze. So I'll put an end to it and move on. It turned out there was an outlaw biker rally in Alpine. What seemed like 2-400 bikers had converged on this town. There were 20 or more staying in the same motel. Turned out the Bandidos were recognized as an outlaw club, and had been suspected of killing a man in Austin a few years ago. They shot him in the head, sniper style, in front of a restaurant. He had been trying to start an Austin chapter of the Hells Angels. We thought if we didn't try that, we'd likely be ok.

Things were quiet as we relaxed a few minutes in the motel room. There were a few groups of them hanging out, drinking beer in front of the rooms of this C-shaped motel.

We went for food. Everything seemed closed in town and seemed to us like they were bracing for a hurricane of drunken bikers. There was a little red burger shack next to a liquor store (Twin Peaks Liquor). Burgers were ordered and we settled on the picnic table, watching bikes pass. We met a local dude in a diesel truck, a Texas standard. He sat with us while he waited for his burger. I don't think we got his name. What he did in his free time was drink beer and weld stuff. We talked about overbearing cops, Big Bend, guitars, and that he had family in Shawno, WI. That seemed about right.

Back at the room, we set to drinking shiner bocks, new belgium pilsners, whiskey, and mozcal-chacmol; Mezcal to be exact. Note to the future; that last one is BAD. Walking down the road, smoking cigarettes a bit later, we talked about what to do next.

We also discussed the complexities of trying to go on a drunk after eating a large meal and a sleepless night. There is a definite wall (word blurred with tequila spill) hit.

"What do you want to do?" we kept asking. Maybe sing songs for money somewhere, maybe climb one of the twin peaks, but I evoked the famous Merle Haggard song, 'I think I'll just sit here and drink.' Then we set back to the motel room and began to climb the walls.

Several more Tequilas later and the bikers seemed to leave town. Things got quiet and Ben passed out spooning his guitar. We woke him up, Blake telling him to come drink and play for the bikers. I told him I needed a better ending to this section. We got him up and went out to mingle.

As it turns out, there were a few different clubs in town. The ones we met were a Mexican outfit called, 'Los Riders'. Their colors were red and gold with patches reading 'LRMC' and 'Red and Gold or Dead and Cold'. I forget their names even now, but the one across from me had a patch that read 'President'.

Though drunk, they seemed rather friendly, giving us some Budwiesers. Ben played some drinking songs, Hank Jr, Pancho & Lefty, some originals. Blake played a bit. Then, in a fit of ballsiness, Ben handed his Taylor over to a drunken Mexican outlaw biker. The risk paid off. He played some traditional Spanish songs. He said he hadn't played in a decade, but played very accurately, Spanish style finger picking, words sung in heartfelt, raspy foreign language, and the message came across.

Sentiment aside, the dude between Ben and I was getting severely drunk. He spoke to me while Ben played, in a very slow deliberate tone. I told him we were from Wisconsin, he was always from Alpine. We gained one point when he didn't know where Wisconsin was. This guy? (blurred with tequila), Manny I think was his name. We'll go with it, it's my story. Manny was half Mexican, half black, and increasingly all drunk. He took issue? with the 'white' view of history at the Alamo, Texas, and the slave trade. I tried carefully to impart on him that I, and not said outwardly that not all white people believes the Davy Crocket version of that tale. It went on and on with that shit back and forth. It felt deep at the time, but now seems drunk. Two drunks not on (Tequilla Damage-Story of my life) the same page. But what in the hell is the real difference? The dude actually cried over the subject. Drunk, like I said.

The last point on that experience; may be culture, maybe alcohol, but Manny couldn't catch sarcasm. I kept trying to make the dude laugh, and didn't once. Many times I would have to assert to him that 'no, I get it.' And he didn't get it that I got it, but I did. We ended that talk, me telling him that we came, we met someone, and we learned something. C'est La Vie.

Finally, back in the room for the night, we recounted what in the hell just happened. I told Blake and Ben that the dude didn't know where Wisconsin was. Shit came to pass, and it came out that Blake did not know where Wisconsin was either... don't tell him I told you.

Rod just told me that he had forgotten to tell you about the part in our discussion where Manny asked "Do you guys know where to get any pussy?"

Rod said "No. It's your town. We didn't bring any with us."

Rod would have written this cloudy memory better, he's really doing a good number writing this trip down. But he just bought a full tank of gas and said he wanted to drive to the other page of the atlas. (No GPS this trip since Ft. Worth).

So we woke up in our delightfully seedy purple painted motel room to the chaos of motorcyclists outside everywhere. 10 AM I busted out Hendrix's Star Spangled Banner on the laptop to wake the guys up. We were in a town literally over-ridden by motorcycle gangs and I was happy as a clam to be in the thick of it.

We checked out at 11am sharp and drove straight south towards Big Bend. Opted to get breakfast down the road. The road did not give us many options. An hour or so later we saw that our highway was adopted by a joint called 'Kathy's Kosmic Kowgirl Kafe'. We all decided that would be a good place to eat. Visions of the bi-cowgirl commune from the Tom Robbins book, 'Even Cowgirls get the Blues" danced through my head. And the place was a bright pink funky trailer of a restaurant. Though the grouchy cowlady who served us was not a hot bi-sexual. Now Blake will pick it up.

I always suspected I was going no where with life, but I'd never thought I'd actually get there until this trip. It has proven to me that no-where is not only a proverbial state of being, but also a reachable one. The automobile that takes you there runs off of beer, the engine needs liquor to keep it lubricated. So long as you don't have a destination, you will get there eventually.

Our plan tonight is to have one of us be the drunkest person in the world. I don't think it will be me, but Rouse is adamant about his idea. Certainly these last few nights weren't aided by the sickening tequila (mezcal), which I believe is the most vile substance on the planet, and possibly a war crime. The bourbon whiskey is much more promising in its unopened glory. It inspires fond memories or lack thereof, of good times.

Like ants on an atlas, we've managed to span the better part of Texas. Yesterday we arrived at the Kosmic Kowgirl Kafe, where we entertained the only other patrons with music and stories. That led us to the camping and hiking we did. I spent the night in the van while Ben and Rod took the tent.

As we left the following morning, we got stopped by Border Patrol. They said the dog smelled drugs, but we weren't kept too long. We are too proud of our <problems(crossed out)> hobby to betray it for less dangerous illegal drugs, and were released by the officer. After some more time on the road, I played some guitar. The exotic scales and progressions were calling my name, and so I indulged. We listened to my band (Fullscore) before stopping by the George W. Bush memorial green road sign of some small town.

Ever since the Invention of the road trip was the tendency to get fucked up and write about it. Hunter S. Thompson, Jack Kerouac, and Woody Guthrie would be proud of us. Many people are going nowhere, but few actually get there.

So it was sitting at the bright pink Kosmic Kathy's Kow-girl Klu Klux whatever, all decked out in it's pink glory, while entertaining and relating stories with some out-doorsy folks our age that we learned that had we taken the interstate to Big Bend, we would have saved 16 hours of driving. But who's counting?

We would later learn that the interstate had 80 mph speed limits- a good time to set the cruise control at 90, and max her out at 94, damn the government... anyway...

"Remember that time you pissed on me?" These are words not to be misquoted. Ben is taking up two beds and no one is getting sleep. He vomited in the bathroom, skillfully, like someone who would save your life if you were drunk to oblivion. He vomits and bounces back to life. Blah. Blah. Ben is the best songwriter I know, this could be his secret, as he pulls his instrument back from his bag.

As if invincible, he rebounds. Authenticity is his trademark. Rouse is the real deal, often over looked, but never under valued.

Blake is too drunk to think.

"We're going to get real coffee on the road. I'm sorry."

It seems a little scattered, has everything been covered up to this point? To make sure; got drunk with 'Los Riders', brisket at kkk cafe: hiked Big Bend, went to Mexico and had a beer, crossed border illegally, threatened with federal prison time, and drove to the next page of the map. Two things to remember, camping is good for vistas in the Chisos Basin, and "It's a good swimming hole, you guys should go there…" said the Border Patrolman, "after I find the mushrooms."

There aren't Border Patrol posts in the park, they are 30 or so miles into Texas on the few roads going to the park. You drive through it, tell them your country of origin, dog smells the car and if they suspect something, they search you.

Based on the condition of the van, I wouldn't have believed anyone riding in there didn't have drugs. They didn't either. Blake and I were essentially detained on the side of the road as they questioned us. The van owner was explaining the situation. Officer Gill said the dog had indicated something in the car. Concealed persons or drugs. He told us that if we had a bag or pipe, we should just give it to him and face the fine, but if he or the dog found it, it would be a federal crime.

So Ben tells the truth. "No drugs here sir. This trip has been a booze trip." But he was a filthy musician and other filthy musicians had ridden in there recently, "So maybe it's residue from that, or maybe it's the bag of mushrooms I had in there last week. The empty bag might still be in there."

"Let's hope not." said Officer Gill as Ben set to tearing apart the van to find the bag. "Just find it, I'm going to have the dog search the car anyway." Ben furiously tore the van apart, explaining to the officer all the weird random shit in the van.

Blake and I, still standing detained, told Gill the nature of our being in that part of the country. That we were now on our way up to Grand Falls to find somewhere to go swimming.

He asked for a map. I told him where in the crime scene to find it. He described a good place to go for that, and while telling me how to get there, forgot that he was a cop, that I was a criminal, and spoke to me like a regular person until he remembered there were drugs to find half way through that quote.

"It's a good swimming hole, you guys should go there... after I find the mushrooms."

A few minutes after that, as if they grew bored of the scene, they said they believed us and let us go without sicking the dog.

Drove north to Marathon. And thus began another. Considered eating there, but I was still all jittery and weirded out by the cop run in. I wanted to put some ground between us.

A couple overlooked side notes: The twigs crawling across the road in Big Bend are actually millipedes. I was accused of being on drugs when I first saw them and tried unsuccessfully to point them out. The last one I saw, I stopped the car and sprinted back to it, hobo knife drawn... the guys followed slowly... not running weather. See I'm not on drugs.

Also... back at the crime scene as I took my guitars out of the car, Gill eyed them up and asked "you guys musicians?"

"Yes, do you want a cd?" I offered. He nodded and I handed him a sampler. He picked it up with two fingers like evidence and gave it to his partner to send to the lab.

I then offered him a Dublin Dr. Pepper as it was hot out, and he said no, that he couldn't accept anything of value. Ouch.

We also missed writing about Big Bend, which was a pretty integral part of our trip to Big Bend.

We set up camp in the basin of a mountain range. Cooler temperatures in the higher elevation. Then drove to Elena Canyon where we hiked along side the Rio Grande and wished we had brought more water. We crossed the Rio into Mexico, opened pints of High Life and gazed back at the motherland. Some tourists walked past on the American side and Blake yelled to them, "Do you need any work done on your house? We work cheap!"

To which the tourists chuckled and replied that he would pick us up at Home Depot tomorrow. Then he took a picture of us and wandered off: Strangers united through the absurdity racism.

We got homesick shortly thereafter and crossed back over to the American side. Back to the campground. Go to the lodge and have a meal. Rod went to work on his homework on the internet. That's right. His homework. What are we 30? And he still hasn't finished his goddamn homework?

Blake flirted with the waitress and lost all his Blake points. Rod did not finish his homework, and we went back to camp to finish the tequila and let the mezcal finish us. Rod wrote in here feverishly, and Blake and I softly played music under the shooting stars.

We drove out the next morning, which was when I saw the millipedes and was accused of being on drugs, and then almost did federal time for having once done drugs and not keeping a clean house. How does that song go? Keep your nose what?

Northward. Stopped at a random diner. Pepitos? Parked Blood Drop next to the sheriffs car. Feeling lucky. Had a distinct uneasy feeling as we entered and all the town folks quieted down and stared at us circa Easy Rider.

Then Rod got gas, and we drove to a cracked little town in the crack of the atlas called Abilene. We tried to find the downtown which took a while, and then when we did we saw we had wasted our time.

Back to the interstates to find a motel. Hit a liquor store on the way. We got ID'd by an older lady, and quickly learned that she had never seen a musician before as she gushed about us looking like movie stars. I gave her an album and she made me sign it, then called her daughter to talk about us as we stood there looking for beer.

She really thought Blake was hot stuff. He probably would have gotten laid had me and Rod tied him up in back of the place and driven away.

At the frontage road, found an American Value Inn. I asked

how much it would cost to stay there, to which they replied how much am I willing to spend. I said 40, so 40 it was.

It was a pretty ritzy room. I almost felt bad that we had it. Fridge, two large beds, a pull-out couch. We started drinking.

Rod finished and sent his homework in at about the same time his teacher e-mailed him an inquiry. Things start getting blurry for me from there. Maybe Rod will take over?

So I couldn't force the journal duty on Rod, and I feel even more inclined to use the cattle Rib on him. From what I can pick up through pictures and conversations. We made a trek for cigarettes after drinking heavily. Then sat on a Texas shaped rock garden as Rod recited some classic stories... at which point I ran back to the room.

When they found me I was either spewing canned clam chowder into the porcelain or not far from it. They got me off the floor, and propped a guitar in my hands. I think Rod tried to give me water and then I purposely dumped it all out on my bed. Then because my bed was wet, I tried to take Rod's bed. The pictures tell me a fight of some sort ensued.

Here's an odd fact- Rod is the only person I trust enough to have drunken fights with. It's an old standing tradition. Sucks for him.-

I think the night ended shortly thereafter, and I passed out in a puddle of what I'm pretty sure was water for the second time this trip. The important thing is that we out drank satan.

Woke up. Hit the Road. Have to get Rod to the airport by 3. Only at the crack in the atlas pages.

Stopped for food in Eastland. Learned it was a dry county. Killed the Mezcal on the highway outside the restaurant. Rod took down the worm. Don't tell him, but that shit is poisonous.

And now here we are. Blake speeding us down I-20 towards Fort Worth, and us planning to do another trip like this again... as soon as we recover from this one... in a year or two.